The Ultimate Indian Instant Pot Cookbook

How To Cook Everything In A Jiffy, Volume 11

Prasenjeet Kumar and Sonali Kumar

Published by Cooking In A Jiffy, 2020.

Table of Contents

Chapter 1: The Age of Instant Pots

It is surprising how the Instant Pot has become nothing short of a phenomenon in such a short time. The device sure looks sleek and futuristic; but we believe its popularity stems more from the fact that it makes both pressure cooking and slow cooking so practical and accessible. You can also use it as a rice cooker, a sauté pan, a steamer, an egg cooker, a sterilizer, and a yogurt maker, if you so wish. Some Instant Pots have buttons for baking too, which makes it a wonderful 9-in-1 cooking appliance equivalent of a Swiss Army knife. And now, some models come with Bluetooth support as well! No wonder, the markets have gone crazy about this convenient, timesaving device that lets you cook almost anything without keeping an eye on the stove.

The traditional way of Indian cooking

Contrast this to the traditional way of cooking Indian cuisine, where the whistle of the non-electric pressure cooker would be the most common sound, you'll often hear in Indian houses. Even now.

So, why do Indians, from slum dwellers to millionaires, love using pressure cookers?

Simply because nothing cooks food faster.

Pressure cookers are fast because they cook at the temperature of steam—at over 120 degree Centigrade (or 248 degree Fahrenheit), and not at the temperature of water that boils around 100 degree Centigrade (or 212 degree Fahrenheit) that open non-pressurized vessels like woks and pans work with.

Just on that count, pressure cookers can be termed "green" because they help save fuel, which in any case is becoming more and more expensive, especially in countries like India. In addition, pressure cookers are considered to preserve nutrition better which is otherwise lost when food is cooked over extended periods of time. Because of these higher temperatures, pressure cookers also kill bacteria and breakdown many a pesticide or chemical that our food may often be contaminated with.

The arrival of Instant Pots

When our path-breaking book *Home Style Indian Cooking In A Jiffy* was first published in 2013, Instant Pots had not become as popular as they are now. At least to my knowledge. Now even the Indian market is full of them with some especially designed for Indian cooking (with designated buttons for *Dal, Idli,* or *Rajma* for example!).

In today's world, there is a big craze for multi-purpose gadgets and Instant Pots seem to just fit that bill so well. Since only one pot functions as a pressure cooker, slow cooker, rice cooker, steamer, and yogurt maker, as we said, it means there is only one pot that is "dirtied" and needs to go into the sink/dishwasher (rather than a pile of pots and pans so typical of cooking Indian cuisine at home).

The biggest advantage Instant Pots have over non-electric pressure cookers is in their ease of use. It is so much easier to push buttons and select a program, just like in a microwave or an oven that you cannot do in a traditional pressure cooker. You can select a program and leave the kitchen, if you so wish, to watch TV or whatever. But you can NEVER ever leave a traditional pressure cooker unattended as it will not switch off on its own.

Instant Pots are also much more user friendly. You don't need the dexterity and practice to make sure that the lid closes well, as required in a traditional pressure cooker.

Nonetheless, when we first used an Instant Pot, my mom (who is the original creator of these recipes, NOT me) was apprehensive that the dishes may not turn out as well as they do in a traditional pressure cooker. But guess what, she was wrong and pleasantly surprised. In fact, if you weren't told about the method of cooking, you wouldn't be able to distinguish the difference in taste between an Indian meal cooked in a traditional pressure cooker versus the same meal cooked in an Instant Pot.

Okay, enough of praising Instant Pots. I am not here to sell the product to you. Nor am I affiliated with any company selling Instant Pots. We wrote this book to meet a very specific need of our readers.

Our other cookbooks (ten of them!) had directions only for using pressure cookers and woks/pans, the traditional ways of cooking Indian food. But when we started getting requests from readers for adding directions for using the Instant Pot for those recipes, we had to listen.

That's why, dear reader, we have come out with this book where we have adapted recipes for some 50 Indian dishes (culled from our other cookbooks) for the Instant Pot. This book, therefore, DOES NOT contain directions for traditional methods of cooking Indian food WITHOUT using Instant Pots. If you do not own an Instant Pot, then you should NOT buy this book. You should then look at the ten other cookbooks (I repeat!) that I have co-authored with my mother and that list you'll find at the end of this book.

As for recommending a good brand of Instant Pot, I'd rather not suggest any, as brands and their reputations vary from country to country. Just pick a brand that meets all your local safety standards, has better consumer reviews, and is manufactured and serviced by a reputed company.

But then this prescription should apply to every gadget that we use in our households every day, shouldn't it?

Chapter 2: Cooking the Indian way

"Tomatoes and oregano make it Italian; wine and tarragon make it French. Sour cream makes it Russian; lemon and cinnamon make it Greek. Soy sauce makes it Chinese; garlic makes it good."–Alice May Brock

Ah, as usual, the lady forgot about the Indian!

Or, maybe she considered the Indian way of matching and mixing unusual flavors too outlandish. After all, where would you find the technique of incorporating more than 10 spices in one dish but in India? Can anyone match the Indian prowess in whipping up an amazing vegetarian meal, even from the most bitter of vegetables (like *karela* or the bitter gourd)?

Displaying an amazing mix of tastes and aromas, Indian cuisine is perhaps the most wonderful, varied, robust, and sensual of all the cuisines in the world. Many celebrity chefs have succeeded in redefining Indian cuisine but without sacrificing its ethnicity. This has no doubt added to the charm and ever-growing popularity of Indian cuisine.

Indian restaurants, within and outside India, are doing a wonderful job of popularizing traditional Indian cooking, but with a contemporary touch, especially in their methods of presentation. For example, many Indian restaurants now serve their cuisines in well engraved woks called *"kadhais"* or in the *"Thali"* in the Indian meal platter format. The interior décor too of these restaurants introduce diners to Indian architecture, heritage, and traditions. Admittedly, this lends a touch of authenticity to the cuisine that is served within the four walls of such restaurants.

Unlike other countries, which have probably 3-4 cuisines at the max, India is a subcontinent with a mixture of numerous culinary traditions. Hence it would be difficult to classify any one regional food of India as representative of the entire Indian cuisine.

Still, if one had to try, I'd say that, in India, there appear to be three distinct ways of cooking. First, the North Indian way that uses *garam masala*, or a medley of aromatic spices like cardamom, cinnamon, cloves, etc. Second, the East Indian way that uses *pachphoran*, or a mixture of five other spices that don't make up *garam masala*. And then, there is the South Indian version that neither uses *garam masala* nor *pachphoran* but displays an original way of cooking by using black mustard seeds, curry leaves, and coconut.

In between we have the Western Indian cuisine which sometimes borrows elements from South India but adds its own unique ingredients, like *Kokum* in the Konkan region, which are not used by any other cuisine in India.

All four versions are absolutely mouth-watering even for veggies. I am sure you can't say the same about most of the Western or even Oriental vegetable dishes, which to the Indian palate tastes like "salad." Unless you use chicken stock or fish sauce to infuse some taste or flavor!

With this brief introduction, I now present 50 mouth-watering Instant Pot-adapted recipes. There are 9 rice recipes, 5 lentils and legumes recipes, 12 recipes for cooking veggies, 6 fish and seafood recipes, and 14 chicken and mutton recipes.

And finally there are 4 desserts you can make from veggies, lentils and legumes. I'm sure you didn't think of that, did you?

So, forget your boring boiled, broiled, and baked ways to make dishes and let this new book open your eyes to the wonderful possibilities of cooking the Indian way—the way Northern, Southern, Eastern, and Western Indians do.

And the bottom line is that you master these, and you can handle any Indian dish from any part of India, I promise.

N.B. Please remember that the "Home Style" recipes I have cataloged here are made regularly in MY home. We strongly encourage you to experiment, adapt, and add your own variation so that the food tastes like YOUR "Home food."

Chapter 3: How is "Home style" Indian food different from "restaurant food?"

Many of my international friends are surprised to learn that there is in India a distinct difference between "Home Style" food and "restaurant food."

"So, what do you Indians eat at home?" They will ask me. "Is it all really so different from 'restaurant food'?"

And, more importantly, is it so superior to "restaurant food" that it deserves to be discussed as a separate category?

I believe that such a "strange" debate among Europeans or Englishmen does not take place in the western world (though I may be wrong!). There you usually look up to the versions created in restaurants and by Michelin Star chefs of say "Roast Turkey" and try to replicate it at home. Here, in India, you almost look down upon the versions of say, "yellow dal" peddled by restaurants and very condescendingly declare your own "Home Style" versions to be less oily or more tasteful and decidedly superior in any case.

I also discovered that certain dishes are just not available in restaurants. For example, I couldn't have my Eastern Indian style *Arhar dal* anywhere in India, including the wayside eateries in Bihar and Uttar Pradesh. Similarly, the *Dahi-Sarson* (yogurt-mustard) fish, which every Bengali household can probably offer, is unavailable even in 5-star hotels in Delhi.

Why, even the simple Indian unleavened bread called *Chapati* or *Phulka*, that I eat every day, would be absent from most restaurant menus who prefer to offer *Tandoori Roti* or *Naan* instead.

Digging a little deeper, I learnt that the whole style of restaurant cooking in India is diametrically opposed to what we practice in our homes with respect to the same dish. For restaurants, speed is of utmost essence as they don't expect any customer to wait for longer than 15 minutes to be served. So they have to keep ingredients ready in a semi-finished condition for a quick conversion in to whatever dish the customer demands. Chicken, for example, will be semi-cooked in a tandoor and then kept ready to be converted into Butter Chicken or Chicken *Tikka* or *Chicken Do Pyaza* (Chicken with two onions literally!) at the drop of a hat. Same goes for the veggies, which will be cut, and even boiled, to be used for any curried or dry version of that vegetable dish. This is the only way restaurants can come up with menus that contain sometimes as many as 100 dishes!

A *dhaba* (roadside eatery) doesn't even have that luxury of a lead time of 15 minutes. Their customers being mostly busy (and burly) truck drivers don't like to wait even for 5 minutes before being served. So a good *dhaba* to survive has to cook and keep simmering its full repertoire of 10-12 dishes all the while. That way it is quite like the "Home Food," which too is fully finished in one go, starting from scratch. The one big difference, however, is that *dhaba* food would contain a lot more oil than home-cooked meals. This is so because oil acts as some kind of preservative for *dhaba* food which, unlike home-cooked meals, doesn't normally go into a fridge.

It was for this reason, it dawned on me, that even the Indian desserts like *Gulab Jamuns* or *Jalebis* served in *dhabas* would be fried!

The upshot of all this very fascinating debate that we carried over many, many moons was the conclusion that there is still a very robust tradition of "Home Style" cuisine alive and kicking in India. And this was very different from Indian restaurant cooking, because:

One, it was cooked from scratch, from fresh ingredients;

Two, many "Home Style" dishes were simply NOT available on restaurant menus;

Three, it was much healthier as it allowed full freedom to change your salt, sugar, and spice levels;

Four, it was not only less oily, but it also permitted you to choose your preferred oil (mustard, olive, coconut, ground nut, soya, sunflower, rice bran, or whatever...), and above all,

Five, it was less complicated and, therefore, easier to cook.

For me, and for all my friends in India, who just couldn't turn into professional chefs overnight, the last point was an eye opener.

"Is that so?" many asked incredulously.

"Prove it, Prasenjeet," someone threw a challenge.

So, I picked up the gauntlet and ventured out to start with a catalog of my own family's "Home Style" Indian cuisine.

And this book is the result of that small, modest attempt to do that.

(Excerpted from my book "Home Style Indian Cooking In A Jiffy" which contains over a-100 Home Style recipes.)

Chapter 4: Rice Recipes

Carbs like rice, wheat, corn, and millets have for centuries occupied a more central position in Indian cuisine than meats. No Indian can think of going to bed after gorging on just a piece of steak, howsoever generous it may be. She will also not be satisfied if some French fries accompanied the steak. For her, the proper accompaniment for a steak or any other meat or vegetable dish would be rice or *rotis*.

And here too, the carbs will have the majority share, at more than 50% on your plate. Of course, at restaurants, you can let your meats (or veggies) occupy this majority position, but no "Home Style" Indian platter would be considered complete without a generous helping of some kind of rice and a roti or both, if possible.

There would, as usual, be mindboggling ways to cook your rice in all kinds of regional flavors and styles. For "Home Style" cooking, however, we present some eight different ways you can cook rice the Indian way in an Instant Pot.

For more rice recipes, please feel free to refer to my book "The Ultimate Guide to Cooking Rice the Indian Way" that has 35 such recipes.

Khichdi (Mixture Dish of Rice, Lentil, and Veggie)

Khichdi literally means a mixture. In some form or another, this is almost compulsorily prepared for the festival of *Makar Sakranti* that is celebrated all over India and Nepal. This festival is also known as *Pongal* in Tamil Nadu, *Bihu* in Assam, *Lohri* in Punjab, or *Uttarayan* in Gujarat.

Interestingly, this is one of the few Hindu festivals that falls on the fixed day of 14 January, when the Sun moves from the Tropic of Capricorn to the Tropic of Cancer heralding the arrival of spring and the beginning of the harvest season.

It is believed that on this day, Lord Surya (the Sun God) visits the house of his son *Shani* (Saturn), who is the lord of the *Makar Rashi* (Capricorn) and the controller of the quantum of misfortune befalling humans. To appease *Shani*, therefore, many Indians prefer cooking *Khichdi* on Saturdays, which is also known as *Shaniwar* or the day of Lord *Shani*.

Khichdi is otherwise the most nutritionally complete dish, consisting of carbs from rice, proteins from legumes and lentils, and vitamins from veggies. Also, it is quite a JIFFY dish.

Serves 3-4

Ingredients

Rice-3/4 cup (approx. 150 grams or 5 oz.)

Moong Dal (Split Bengal Gram)-1/4 cup (approx. 50 grams or 1.75 oz.)

Onion-1 (chopped)

Ginger-1-inch (2.5 cm or 1/3rd length of a finger) piece

Spinach (only leaves)-500 grams or 18oz or 2 cups coarsely chopped

Peas–100 grams (half cup or 3.5 oz)

Carrots-2 (cut into small pieces)

Tomato-1

Khada (that is, whole and not powdered) *Garam Masala* (Green cardamom–2, brown cardamom-1, Bay leaves-2, cinnamon stick-1/2 inch, black pepper-6, cloves-4, cumin seeds-1/2 tea spoon)

Coriander (*Dhania*) powder-1 teaspoon

Red chilli powder -1/4 teaspoon (just for flavor and not to make it hot; you can add more if you like it hot)

Turmeric (*Haldi*)-1 teaspoon

Asafoetida (*Hing*)-1/4 teaspoon

Ghee (clarified butter)-2 tablespoon full

Salt- 1 level teaspoon or to taste.

Water-3 cups (This will give your *Khichdi* a wet consistency. However, if you like your *Khichdi* to be drier, then add only 2 cups of water.)

Method

Wash the rice and *dal* together and let it dry for 5 minutes on an inclined plate.

Turn on the Instant Pot.

Press the sauté button and take it to high.

Add the *ghee* in the inner pot.

When the *ghee* warms up, add the *Khada Garam Masala* and Asafoetida.

Let these all crackle but NOT burn.

Now add the onion and ginger.

Sauté this for 2 minutes and then add the peas and the carrots.

Stir well.

Now add the coarsely chopped spinach, turmeric, coriander powder, red chilli powder, and salt.

Add the rice, *dal,* and the tomatoes.

Stir well.

Add the water and close the lid. Press the rice button. Otherwise, pressure cook for 5 minutes. And let it cool naturally.

That's all. Your *Khichdi* is ready.

Prep time: 5 minutes

Cooking time: 10 minutes

Total time: 15 minutes

Note: Different Instant Pot models may have different designs or control options, so please feel free to adapt as you deem fit.

Mattar Pulao (Peas Rice)

This is the simplest pilaf dish that you can prepare in a JIFFY.

Serves 3-4

Ingredients

Long grain rice (Basmati)-1 cup (approx. 200 grams or 7 oz.)

Peas-1/2 cup (approx. 100 grams or 3.5 oz.)

Sliced Onion-1 (Medium)

Water-2 cups

Cumin seeds (*Jeera*)-1/2 teaspoon

Green cardamom (*Chhoti elaichi*)-2

Cinnamon (*Dalchini*)-1/2 inch

Cloves (*Laung*)-4

Bay leaf (*Tejpatta*)-1

Clarified butter (*Ghee*)-2 tablespoon

Salt–1/2 tea spoon or to taste

Sugar-1/4 teaspoon

Method

Wash the rice well (in a vessel 3-4 times, but don't rub it lest the grains break), and let it "dry" naturally, on an inclined plate, for 15-20 minutes. This helps enhance the aroma.

Turn on the Instant Pot.

Press the sauté button and take it to high.

Add *ghee* in the inner pot.

When the *ghee* warms up, add the cumin seeds along with the cardamom, cinnamon, cloves, and bay leaves.

As soon as it all starts giving off a pleasant aroma, in less than a minute, add the onion slices, and fry till translucent.

Do please make sure that the spices brown and not burn, otherwise your dish will be ruined.

Add the peas and stir for a minute.

Now add the rice along with the salt and sugar.

Stir well.

Add the water.

Close the lid and press the rice button. Otherwise, pressure cook for 5 minutes. And let it cool naturally.

That's all. Your aromatic Pea *Pulao* is ready.

Prep time: 7 minutes

Cooking time: 10 minutes

Total time: 17 minutes

Note: Different Instant Pot models may have different designs or control options, so please feel free to adapt as you deem fit.

Dry Fruits Pulao

This is a rich pilaf dish, fit enough to be on a grand Moghul's table.

Serves 3-4

Ingredients

Long grain rice (Basmati)-1 cup

Water-2 cups

Black cumin seeds (*Shahi Jeera*)-1/2 teaspoon

Green cardamom (*Chhoti elaichi*)-2

Saffron - few strands dissolved in ¼ cup milk

Raisins-2 tablespoon

Blanched almonds-3 tablespoon

(To blanch almonds, immerse them in half a cup of hot water for 30 minutes. Remove the skin thereafter.)

Cashew nuts-3 tablespoon

Clarified butter (*Ghee*)-1 tablespoon

Salt—1 teaspoon or to taste

Sugar-1/4 teaspoon

Method

Wash the rice well (*in a vessel 3-4 times, but don't rub it lest the grains break*), and let it naturally "dry," on an inclined plate, for 15-20 minutes. This helps enhance the aroma.

Turn on the Instant Pot.

Press the sauté button and take it to high.

In the inner pot, add the clarified butter.

When the butter warms up, add the cumin seeds along with the green cardamom and cashew nuts.

As soon as it all starts giving off a pleasant aroma, in less than a minute, add the rice along with the salt and sugar. Do please make sure that the spices brown and not burn, otherwise your dish will be spoiled.

Add the raisins and the blanched almonds.

Stir well.

Add the water and saffron dissolved in milk.

Close the lid and press the rice button. Otherwise, pressure cook for 5 minutes. And let it cool naturally.

That's all. Your hot fluffy Dry Fruits *Pulao* is ready.

Prep time: 7 minutes

Cooking time: 10 minutes

Total time: 17 minutes

Note: Different Instant Pot models may have different designs or control options, so please feel free to adapt as you deem fit.

Kashmiri Sweet Pulao

This is a really sweet dish from a really sweet place that many declare as the "Paradise on Earth."

Serves 3-4

Ingredients

Long grain rice (Basmati)-1 cup

Water-2 cups

Cinnamon—1 stick powdered

Saffron - few strands dissolved in ¼ cup milk

Raisins-1 tablespoon

Candied Cherries—2 tablespoon

Candied Ginger (Chopped)—1 tablespoon

Candied Orange Peel (Chopped)—1 tablespoon

Cashew nuts—2 tablespoon

Clarified butter (*Ghee*)-1 tablespoon

Salt—1 teaspoon or to taste

Method

Wash the rice well (*in a vessel 3-4 times, but don't rub it lest the grains break*), and let it naturally dry, on an inclined plate, for 15-20 minutes. This helps enhance the aroma.

Turn on the Instant Pot.

Press the sauté button and take it to high.

In the inner pot, add the clarified butter.

When the butter warms up, add the cashew nuts till they acquire a light golden color.

Add the rice along with all the remaining ingredients, except saffron.

Stir well. Now add the water and saffron dissolved in milk.

Close the lid and press the rice button. Otherwise, pressure cook for 5 minutes. And let it cool naturally.

That's all. Your Kashmiri Sweet *Pulao* is ready.

Prep time: 7 minutes

Cooking time: 10 minutes

Total time: 17 minutes

Note: Different Instant Pot models may have different designs or control options, so please feel free to adapt as you deem fit.

Mixed Vegetable Biryani

Who says vegetarians can't enjoy *Biryanis*? Try this dish, and I guarantee you the same flavors as of any normal non-vegetarian *Biryani*.

Serves 5-6

Ingredients

Long grain rice (Basmati)-2 cups

Peas-1/4 cup

Carrots cut into small pieces-1/4 cup

Cauliflower florets-1/4 cup

French Beans-1/4 cup

Blanched Almonds-2 tablespoon

(To blanch almonds, immerse them in half a cup of hot water for 30 minutes. Remove the skin thereafter.)

Sliced Onion-1 (Medium)

Chopped Ginger-1-inch piece

Chopped Garlic-4 cloves

Turmeric (*Haldi*)-1/2 teaspoon

Red chilli powder-1/4 teaspoon (just for flavor and not to make it hot; you can add more if you like it hot)

Coriander powder-1 teaspoon

Garam Masala (a mixture of common Indian spices) -1/2 teaspoon

Tip: If you can't get ready-made *garam masala* mixture from a nearby Indian store, you can make yours by using 1 black cardamom, 3 green cardamoms, 4 cloves, and 1-inch cinnamon—all ground together for this dish.

Red Tomatoes pureed-2

Cumin seeds (*Jeera*)-1/2 teaspoon

Clarified butter (*Ghee*)-4 tablespoon

Salt to taste

Sugar-1/4 teaspoon

Water-4 cups

Method

Wash the rice well (*in a vessel 3-4 times, but don't rub it lest the grains break*), and let it naturally dry, on an inclined plate, for 15-20 minutes. This helps enhance the aroma.

Turn on the Instant Pot.

Press the sauté button and take it to high.

In the inner pot, add the clarified butter.

When the butter warms up, add the cumin seeds. As soon as it starts giving off a pleasant aroma, in less than a minute, add the onion slices, and fry till translucent. Do please make sure that the spices brown and not burn, otherwise your dish will be spoiled.

Add the ginger and garlic. Stir for a minute.

Add all the vegetables and stir well.

Now add the turmeric, chilli powder, coriander, and *garam masala* and again stir well.

Pour the tomato puree over this mixture and stir till the tomatoes give off a nice aroma. That's the indication that they are getting cooked.

Add now the blanched almonds.

Add the salt and sugar. Now add the rice.

Stir well.

Add the water.

Close the lid and press the rice button. Otherwise, pressure cook for 5 minutes. And let it cool naturally.

That's all. Your Vegetable *biryani* is ready.

This is a complete meal in itself.

Prep time: 7 minutes

Cooking time: 10 minutes

Total time: 17 minutes

Note: Different Instant Pot models may have different designs or control options, so please feel free to adapt as you deem fit.

Mutton Biryani

This is for the carnivore who has to have his meat. If you want to pair your meats with rice, however, this could be the tastiest way to do that.

Serves 5-6

Ingredients

Long grain rice (Basmati)-2 cups

For the rice:

Salt—1/2 teaspoon

Sugar—1/2 teaspoon

Ghee (Clarified butter)—1 teaspoon

Other ingredients:

Mutton pieces-1 kg (2 lbs) (4 cups)

Onions-3 large chopped

Ginger-2-inch piece chopped

Garlic-8 cloves chopped

Tomatoes-3 chopped

Coriander (Dhania) powder-2 teaspoon

Turmeric powder-1 teaspoon

Garam Masala-1 teaspoon

Tip: If you can't get ready-made garam masala mixture from a nearby Indian store, you can make yours by using 1 black cardamom, 3 green cardamoms, 4 cloves, and 1-inch cinnamon—all ground together for this dish.

Red chilli powder-1/4 teaspoon (just for flavor and not to make it hot; you can add more if you like it hot)

Cumin seeds (Jeera)-1/2 teaspoon

Tomato Ketchup-2 tablespoon

Red Tomatoes pureed-2

Cooking Oil-3 tablespoon

Ghee (Clarified butter)-1 tablespoon

Water-4 cups

Salt- 1 + ½ teaspoon or to taste

Method

Wash the rice well (*in a vessel 3-4 times, but don't rub it lest the grains break*), and let it naturally dry, on an inclined plate, for 15-20 minutes. Sprinkle the salt and sugar on the rice and gently stir in the *ghee*. Keep aside. This all will help enhance the taste and aroma.

Switch on the Instant Pot and press the sauté button.

In the inner pot, add the oil.

As the oil turns hot, add the cumin seeds, and let them splutter.

Immediately add the chopped onion.

Stir well till the onions become translucent.

Now, add the chopped ginger and garlic, and stir till it all starts giving off a pleasant aroma.

Add the mutton pieces and the *ghee* (clarified butter).

Stir well.

Add the coriander powder, turmeric, garam masala, and red chilli powder.

Stir the mutton till all the water evaporates, and the mutton becomes almost dry. This process ensures that all the raw flavors of mutton, onions, etc. are removed.

Add now the tomatoes, the ketchup, and the puree.

Stir well again and add the salt.

Let the tomatoes cook well.

Now, add the water, and switch off the sauté button.

Close the lid and press the meat/lamb/curry button or pressure cook for 20 minutes.

Release the pressure.

Open the lid and add the rice. Gently stir.

Close the lid and press the rice button or pressure cook for 5 minutes.

That's all. Your mouth-watering Mutton Biryani is now ready.

Prep time: 7 minutes

Cooking time: 40 minutes

Total time: 47 minutes

Note: Different Instant Pot models may have different designs or control options, so please feel free to adapt as you deem fit.

Chicken Keema Biryani

This is for that carnivore who prefers his meat to be white, but doesn't want to compromise on the flavors and taste.

Serves 5-6

Ingredients

Long grain rice (Basmati)-2 cups

For the rice:

Salt—1/2 teaspoon

Sugar—1/2 teaspoon

Ghee (Clarified butter)—1 teaspoon

Other ingredients:

Chicken mince—1/2 kg (500 grams or 18oz or 2 cups)

Medium-size Onions—2 (chopped)

Garlic-4 pieces

Ginger-1-inch

Fresh tomato-2 (chopped)

Red Tomatoes pureed-2

Turmeric (*Haldi*) - 1/2 tea spoon

Dry crushed coriander (*Dhania*)-2 tea spoon

Garam Masala (mixture of common Indian spices) crushed- 1/2 tea spoon

Tip: If you can't get ready-made *garam masala* mixture from a nearby Indian store, you can make yours by using 1 black cardamom, 3 green cardamoms, 4 cloves, and 1- inch cinnamon—all ground together for this dish.

Kashmiri Red chilli powder—1/4 tea spoon (Recommended for color, but if you like your dish to be spicy, use any other red chilli powder)

Yogurt unsweetened (Indian set curd is preferred)-1 table spoon

Cumin whole (Jeera)-1/2 tea spoon

Salt-1/2 tea spoon (or to taste)

Tomato Ketchup-1 table spoon

Cooking oil-1 table spoon

Ghee (clarified butter)-1 tea spoon

Water-1 tea cup

Method

Wash the rice well (*in a vessel 3-4 times, but don't rub it lest the grains break*), and let it naturally dry, on an inclined plate, for 15-20 minutes. Sprinkle the salt and sugar on the rice and gently stir in the *ghee*. Keep aside. This all will help enhance the taste and aroma.

Blend together (in a blender preferably!) the onions, garlic, ginger, and tomatoes to a fine paste.

Switch on the Instant Pot and press the sauté button.

Heat the oil in the inner pot.

Add cumin seeds to the oil and as they turn brown, add the paste from the blender and gently fry.

As the paste starts giving off a pleasant aroma, add the chicken mince, and sauté gently.

Add all the dry *garam masala*, salt, and curd to this mixture and keep stirring till they start becoming almost dry.

Add the tomato ketchup and puree to the mixture and stir again.

At this juncture, add the *ghee* for a lovely taste.

Now, add the water, and switch off the sauté button. Close the lid of the inner pot, and pressure cook for 5 minutes.

Release the pressure.

Open the lid and add the rice. Gently stir.

Close the lid and press the rice button or pressure cook for 5 minutes.

That's all. Your Chicken *Keema Biryani* is ready.

Prep time: 7 minutes

Cooking time: 10 minutes

Total time: 17 minutes

Note: Different Instant Pot models may have different designs or control options, so please feel free to adapt as you deem fit.

Pongal

This is the South Indian Khichdi, and a very tasty variation of its North Indian cousin! This is also a festival dish that is compulsorily prepared in Tamil Nadu on *Pongal* or *Makar Sakranti* when the Sun moves from the Tropic of Capricorn to the Tropic of Cancer heralding the arrival of spring and the beginning of the harvest season.

Serves 3-4

Ingredients

Rice-3/4 cup (approx. 150 grams or 5 oz.)

Moong Dal (Split Bengal Gram)-1/4 cup (approx. 50 grams or 1.75 oz.)

Ginger-1-inch (2.5 cm or 1/3rd length of a finger) piece

Turmeric (*Haldi*)-1 teaspoon

Asafoetida (*Hing*)-1/4 teaspoon

Ghee (clarified butter)-2 tablespoon full

Salt- 1 level teaspoon or to taste.

Water-3 cups

Method

Wash the rice and *dal* together and let it dry for 5 minutes on an inclined plate.

Turn on the Instant Pot.

Press the sauté button and take it to high.

Add *ghee* in the inner pot.

When the *ghee* warms up, add the Asafoetida (*Hing*) and ginger.

Let this brown but NOT burn.

Now add the rice, *dal*, turmeric, and the salt.

Stir well.

Add the water. Close the lid and press the rice button. Otherwise, pressure cook for 5 minutes. And let it cool naturally.

That's all. Your *Pongal* is ready.

Prep time: 5 minutes

Cooking time: 10 minutes

Total time: 15 minutes

Note: Different Instant Pot models may have different designs or control options, so please feel free to adapt as you deem fit.

Sweet Pongal

Another festival dish from the South Indian state of Tamil Nadu.

Serves 3-4

Ingredients

Rice-3/4 cup (approx. 150 grams or 5 oz.)

Moong Dal (Split Bengal Gram)-1/4 cup (approx. 50 grams or 1.75 oz.)

Jaggery (*Gur* which is unprocessed sugar)-1 cup (approx. 200 grams or 7 oz.)

Roasted Cashew nuts-2 tablespoon fried golden and then chopped up.

Note: To fry the cashew nuts, add about a tablespoon of cooking oil in a small pan. Put the pan on your heat source. When the oil heats up, add the cashew nuts, and stir till they turn golden. Immediately remove the cashew nuts to a plate and chop. Remember, if you leave the cashew nuts in the pan, the hot oil will keep roasting the cashew nuts and may burn them.

Ghee (clarified butter)-2 tablespoon

Water-3 cups

Method

Wash the rice and *dal* together and let it dry for 5 minutes on an inclined plate.

Turn on the Instant Pot.

Press the sauté button and take it to high.

Add *ghee* in the inner pot.

When the *ghee* warms up, add the rice and lentils.

Stir well.

Add 2 cups of water. Close the lid and press the rice button. Otherwise, pressure cook for 5 minutes. And let it cool naturally.

Meanwhile, in a pan melt the jaggery with 1 cup water, and let it come to a boil.

Open the Instant Pot and press the sauté button.

Add the boiled jaggery to it along with the roasted cashew nuts.

Mix well.

That's all. Your Sweet *Pongal* is ready.

Prep time: 5 minutes

Cooking time: 10 minutes

Total time: 15 minutes

Note: Different Instant Pot models may have different designs or control options, so please feel free to adapt as you deem fit.

Chapter 5: Dal (Lentil and Legumes) Recipes

Call them soups or curries, but you will find *dals* in almost every home in India.

Vir Sanghvi[1], the noted Indian columnist and gourmand, calls *"Dals the great unifier of India."*

Dals are spiced or tempered in as many ways as there are regions and languages in India. But the common thread would be that, as sources of excellent vegetarian protein, they should be on every Indian's platter.

Vir Sanghvi explains that when *"you talk to foreigners about Indian food, you run into all kinds of misconceptions about what constitutes the essence of Indian cuisine. When I was studying abroad, I was forever being asked, 'Do you miss curry?' These days it is more likely to be 'Longing for a bit of tandoori chicken, eh?'*

In reality, I've never met an Indian who thinks of his own cuisine in terms of tandoori chicken, a restaurant dish that we rarely eat at home. Nor do I know many Indians who stay awake at nights, when they are away from home, pining for rogan josh or chicken shahi korma or any other kind of curry.

What we do miss is something that foreigners rarely understand.

We miss dal.

---

1. http://www.virsanghvi.com/Article-Details.aspx?key=586

I know grown men who get dal cravings when they have been away from India for long stretches. At University, I knew students who missed the taste of home-cooked dal. And even now, if you ask most Indians what it is that constitutes the heart of real Indian food (the kind that Mummy makes) the answer is nearly always framed in terms of dal."

Touché. I couldn't agree more.

In this backdrop, I shall now present the most popular "Home Style" *dal* (and curry) recipes, using *Arhar/Toor Dal* (Split Pigeon Peas), *Moong Dal* (Bengal Gram), *Chhola* (Whole Chickpea), Sambar, and *Rajma* (Red Kidney Beans).

For more lentil and legume recipes, please feel free to refer to my book "The Ultimate Guide to Cooking Lentils the Indian Way" that has 58 such recipes.

Arhar Dal (Split Pigeon Peas)

This is the staple North Indian *dal*, especially for the people of Bihar or Uttar Pradesh.

Serves 3-4

Ingredients

Arhar/Toor (Split Pigeon Peas) *Dal*-1/2 small cup (approx. 100 grams or 3.5 oz.)

Water-4 small cups (same cup as above!)

Turmeric (*Haldi*) powder-1/2 tea spoon

Salt–1/2 tea spoon or to taste

Tomato–1

Cumin seeds (*Jeera*)–1/2 tea spoon

Ghee (clarified butter)-1 tea spoon

Fresh Coriander (*Dhania*) leaves (optional)

Method

Wash the *Arhar Dal* well in a vessel 3-4 times.

Turn on the Instant Pot.

Press the sauté button and take it to high.

Add the *ghee* in the inner pot.

When the *ghee* warms up, add the cumin seeds, and let these splutter. Please ensure that the cumin doesn't burn and only turns brown.

Now add the washed *Arhar Dal* along with water, turmeric, salt, and chopped tomato.

Close the lid, and pressure cook for six minutes. Let it cool down naturally.

That's all. Your simple *Arhar Dal* is ready.

If you prefer your *dal* to have a thicker (restaurant-style) consistency, you can put it back on sauté without the lid and let the excess water evaporate. While doing that, please remember to keep stirring, so that the *dal* does not burn.

If you want, you may add some chopped fresh coriander leaves and serve.

Prep time: 5 minutes for washing and collecting all ingredients

Cooking time: 10 minutes

Total time: 15 minutes

Note: Different Instant Pot models may have different designs or control options, so please feel free to adapt as you deem fit.

Moong Dal Dhuli (Split Bengal Gram): Bengali style

Serves 3-4

Ingredients

Dhuli Moong (Split Bengal Gram) *Dal*-1/2 cup (approx. 100 grams or 3.5 oz.)

Water-4 cups (same cup as above!)

Turmeric (*Haldi*) powder-1/2 tea spoon

Salt–1/2 tea spoon or to taste

Sugar- ¼ tea spoon

Desiccated coconut - 2 tea spoons

Garam Masala- ½ tea spoon

Tip: If you can't get ready-made *garam masala* mixture from a nearby Indian store, you can make yours by using 1 black cardamom, 3 green cardamoms, 4 cloves, and 1-inch cinnamon—all ground together for this dish.

Tomato—2

Onion (chopped) - 1

Garlic (chopped)–2 cloves

Ginger (chopped) - 1-inch (2.5 cm or 1/3rd length of a finger) piece

Cumin seeds (*Jeera*)–1/2 tea spoon

Ghee (clarified butter)-2 tea spoons

Fresh Coriander (optional)

Method

Turn on the Instant Pot.

Press the sauté button, and take it to high.

Take the *Moong Dal,* and put it in the Instant Pot, **without washing**.

Dry roast the *Moong Dal* till it turns a nice golden brown color.

Switch off the Instant Pot.

Remove the *Moong Dal, wash it* and keep it aside. (The Moong Dal will not roast properly if you have washed it and made it wet. That's why you have to roast the Moong Dal first and then wash it.)

Again, turn on the Instant Pot.

Press the sauté button, and take it to high.

Add the *ghee* in the inner pot.

As soon as the *ghee* warms up, add the cumin seeds.

Let it splutter, which takes a few seconds only. Please ensure that the cumin doesn't burn and only turns brown.

Now add the onion, garlic, and ginger and stir till the onions become translucent.

Now add the *Moong Dal* (roasted and washed), desiccated coconut, *garam masala*, sugar, turmeric, salt, tomato, and water.

Close the lid, and pressure cook for three minutes.

Let it cool down naturally.

That's all. Your *Moong Dal*-Bengali style is ready.

If you prefer your *dal* to have a thicker (restaurant-style) consistency, you can put it back on sauté without the lid and let the excess water evaporate. While doing that, please remember to keep stirring, so that the *dal* does not burn.

If you want, you may add some chopped fresh coriander leaves to it and serve.

Prep time: 7 minutes for washing and collecting all ingredients

Cooking time: 5 minutes

Note: Different Instant Pot models may have different designs or control options, so please feel free to adapt as you deem fit.

Rajma (Red Kidney Beans curry)

A perennial favorite of the North Indian states of Punjab, Haryana, Himachal Pradesh, and Jammu & Kashmir, this dish is cooked more like meat than lentils. Many wayside eateries or *dhabas* thrive on serving just *Rajma* with fragrant Basmati rice and readily find a seemingly never-ending queue of diners.

Try this dish once, and you will not touch that can of insipid Baked Beans with tomato sauce ever again!

Serves 3-4

Ingredients

Red Kidney beans (*Rajma*)-1 small cup (approx. 100 grams or 3.5 oz.)

Water-4 cups (same cup as above!)

Chopped Onion-1

Chopped Garlic-5 cloves

Chopped Ginger-1-inch (2.5 cm or 1/3rd length of a finger) piece

Chopped Tomatoes-4

Garam Masala powder-1/2 teaspoon

Tip: If you can't get ready-made *garam masala* mixture from a nearby Indian store, you can make yours by using 1 black

cardamom, 3 green cardamoms, 4 cloves, and 1-inch cinnamon—all ground together for this dish.

Turmeric (*Haldi*)-1/2 teaspoon

Cumin seeds (*Jeera*)-1/2 teaspoon

Kashmiri red chilli powder-1/2 teaspoon (just for flavor and not to make it hot; you can add more if you like it hot)

Clarified butter (*Ghee*)-2 tablespoon

Salt–1/2 tea spoon or to taste

Sugar-1/4 teaspoon

Method

Soak the kidney beans overnight in 2 cups of water.

Note: Remember if you don't pre-soak the kidney beans, the cooking time will be extremely long and the beans may not cook that easily.

Turn on the Instant Pot.

Press the sauté button, and take it to high.

Add the *ghee* in the inner pot, and when it warms up, add the cumin seeds.

As soon as the cumin seeds turn brown, which takes just a few seconds (do please make sure they don't burn), add the chopped onion, garlic, and ginger.

Sauté well till the onions become translucent and start giving off a pleasant aroma.

Add the kidney beans, along with the chilli powder, turmeric powder, *garam masala*, salt, and sugar.

Sauté for about a minute.

To this mixture, now add the tomatoes.

Roast well till the tomatoes are cooked.

Now add 4 cups of water, close the lid, and pressure cook for thirty minutes. Let it cool down naturally.

Alternatively, you can press the chilli bean button on your Instant Pot, if there be one.

Open the lid and see if the *Rajma* has the desired consistency. In case you want it to be more wet, you can add some more water. In case you want it drier, then you can put it back on sauté without the lid and let the excess water evaporate. While doing either, please remember to keep stirring, so that the *Rajma* does not burn.

This dish tastes delicious with plain, long grain Basmati rice.

Prep time: Soak overnight. After that, prep time should be about 5 minutes for washing and collecting all ingredients.

Cooking time: 35 minutes

Total time: 40 minutes

Note: Different Instant Pot models may have different designs or control options, so please feel free to adapt as you deem fit.

Chhola (Whole Chickpea Curry)

This is another classic dish of the North Indian states of Punjab, Haryana, Himachal Pradesh, and Jammu & Kashmir. Again, like *Rajma*, this dish too is cooked more like meat than lentils. However, unlike *Rajma* which is traditionally enjoyed with fragrant Basmati rice, *Chhola* is paired more with *Pooris* (fried and puffed up Indian unleavened bread) and *Bhathuras* (fried and puffed up Indian leavened bread). This combo is in fact quite a *favorite* for breakfasts or rather brunches.

Try this dish with rice or any kind of bread, Western or Indian, and I bet you will fall in love with it.

Serves 3-4

Ingredients

Whole white Chickpea (*Kabuli Chana* or *Chhola*)-1 small cup (approx. 200 grams or 7 oz.)

Onions-2

Garlic-6 cloves

Ginger-1+1/2 inches (4 cm or 2/3rd length of a finger) piece

Tomatoes-3

Cumin seeds (*Jeera*)-1/2 teaspoon

Coriander powder (*Dhania*)-2 teaspoon

Turmeric (*Haldi*)- 1 teaspoon

Garam Masala powder-1/2 teaspoon

Tip: If you can't get ready-made *garam masala* mixture from a nearby Indian store, you can make yours by using 1 black cardamom, 3 green cardamoms, 4 cloves, and 1- inch cinnamon—all ground together for this dish.

Kashmiri Red Chilli powder-1/2 teaspoon (just for flavor and not to make it hot; you can add more if you like it hot)

Cooking Oil- 2 tablespoon

Salt–1/2 tea spoon or to taste

Method

Soak the chickpeas in a vessel with water (which covers the chickpeas completely) at least for 4 hours. This way when you cook the chickpeas, they become nice and tender and take less time to cook.

In a grinder, make a fine paste of the tomatoes, ginger, garlic, and onion.

Turn on the Instant Pot.

Press the sauté button, and take it to high.

Add the cooking oil in the inner pot.

When the oil warms up, add the cumin seeds.

In a few seconds, as soon as the cumin seeds turn brown, add the paste you have just made in the grinder. Do please ensure that the cumin seeds do not burn.

Sauté the paste till it starts giving off a pleasant aroma.

Now add the turmeric powder, *garam masala,* red chilli powder, coriander powder, and salt.

Sauté for another 2 minutes.

Now add the pre-soaked chickpeas with enough water to cover the chickpeas. Pressure cook for 30 minutes. Let it cool down naturally.

Alternatively, you can press the chilli bean button on your Instant Pot, if there be one.

In case you want the curry to be more wet, you can add some more water. In case you want it drier, then you can put it back on sauté without the lid and let the excess water evaporate. While doing either, please remember to keep stirring, so that the chickpea does not burn.

That's all. Your *Chhola* is ready.

Prep time: Soak overnight, or at least for 4 hours. After that prep time should be 5 minutes for washing and collecting all ingredients.

Cooking time: 35 minutes

Total time: 40 minutes

Note 1: Different Instant Pot models may have different designs or control options, so please feel free to adapt as you deem fit.

Note 2: If you have sampled *Chhola* in a *dhaba* (wayside eatery), you may find my "Home Style" recipe a little mild. This is for two major reasons. First, since the *dhabas* have to cook enormous quantities (say 10 kgs or 22 lbs of chickpeas in one go), and that too in big non-pressurized vessels, they slip in some baking soda to their pre-soaking process. I'm not in favor of this practice because this unnecessarily increases the sodium levels of your *Chhola* (which is bad for your blood pressure) without enhancing the taste. In fact, the somewhat soapy taste that baking soda imparts to this dish may not suit sensitive palates.

Which leads to the second point of drowning this baking soda induced flavor. This is done by using stronger spices like *Kastoori Methi* (fragrant Fenugreek). Then *Anardana* (ground seeds of wild pomegranate) is used to increase the tanginess of the dish. Finally, used tea leaves are added to impart a blackish color to the *Chhola*.

I have nothing against the second point. Use it if you crave the authentic *dhaba* flavor.

But for the first, you may be better off using a pressure cooker or a slow cooker or an Instant Pot than using baking soda!

Sambar

The South Indian states of Andhra Pradesh, Tamil Nadu, Karnataka, and Kerala prefer to cook their *Arhar/Toor dal* with this fiery but tasty twist. In fact, they love *Sambar* so much that they have to have it for all their meals–breakfast, lunch, and dinner!

Be careful, this is NOT a mild lentil soup.

Serves 3-4

Ingredients

Arhar/Toor (Split Pigeon Peas) *Dal*-1 small cup (approx. 200 grams or 7 oz.)

Water-4 cups (same cup as above!)

Onion-1

Tomatoes-2

Garlic-6 cloves

French Beans-100 grams (3.5oz) (half cup)

Pumpkin-100 grams (3.5oz) (half cup)

Bottle Gourd-100 grams (3.5oz) (half cup)

Sambar masala powder-4 teaspoon

Tip: If you can't get ready-mix Sambar masala powder from a nearby store or find it too spicy, you can make yours by mixing together: 1 teaspoon *Chana Dal* (Split Chickpea), 1 teaspoon *Urad Dal* (Black Lentils), 1 tablespoon *Dhania* (whole coriander) seeds, ½ teaspoon *Kali Mirch* (black pepper corns), ½ teaspoon *Methi* (fenugreek) seeds, ½ teaspoon *Hing* (Asafoetida), 1 teaspoon *Jeera* (cumin seeds), 1 dry red chilli whole (optional, if you don't mind the heat!). Dry roast them for a minute. Then grind (in a mixer-grinder) and store in an airtight jar.

Tamarind paste-1 tablespoon dissolved in 1/2 cup of water

Ghee (Clarified butter)-1 tablespoon

Black Mustard seeds (*Rai*)-1 teaspoon

Curry leaves-10-12

Salt–1/2 tea spoon or to taste

Sugar-1/2 teaspoon

Method

Wash the *dal* and vegetables well.

Chop up the vegetables, onion, tomatoes, and garlic.

Turn on the Instant Pot.

Press the sauté button, and take it to high.

Add the *ghee* in the inner pot.

When the *ghee* warms up, add the black mustard seeds, and the curry leaves. Let the seeds splutter.

Now add the *dal* and the chopped vegetables along with the chopped onion, tomatoes, and garlic.

Add the *sambar* masala, salt, and sugar.

Add water.

Close the lid, and pressure cook for ten minutes. Let it cool down naturally.

When the Instant Pot has cooled down, open the lid, and add the tamarind paste.

Press the sauté button, and boil it once more without covering it with the lid.

That's all. Your *Sambar* is ready.

In case you cannot get curry leaves, black mustard seeds alone too can impart the required flavor.

If you like your *Sambar* to taste more sour, you can add more tamarind paste. Similarly, if you want your *Sambar* to taste sweeter, you can add more sugar.

Prep time: 8 minutes for washing, chopping, and collecting all ingredients

Cooking time: 12 minutes

Total time: 20 minutes

Note: Different Instant Pot models may have different designs or control options, so please feel free to adapt as you deem fit.

Chapter 6: Veggie Recipes

"Many people are turned off at eating vegetarian because of the misconception that all dishes are just an arrangement of bland vegetables." –Marcus Samuelsson

But probably Marcus was not referring to veggies cooked the Indian way. Because if he did, he would have to acknowledge that no one cooks vegetables as well and in as many ways as the Indians do.

For pure vegetarians, India is just heaven.

There is a myth that Indians cannot have anything dry, that they have to have curries in all their meals. So much so that in Britain, many Indian restaurants are simply called "Curry Houses."

Well, nothing could be farther from the truth. You'll be surprised to know Indians love "dry" dishes regardless of whether they already have a curry on their meal platter (*Thali*) or not. In fact, it is almost compulsory to have a curry balanced by a dry dish.

It is in that background that we present both ways of cooking vegetables the Indian Way—dry as well as curries.

There are in all 12 outstanding "Home Style" vegetable dishes—5 dry and 7 curries, that you should love experimenting with in your Instant Pot.

For more veggie recipes, please feel free to refer to my book "The Ultimate Guide to Cooking Vegetables the Indian Way" that has 101 such recipes.

Palak Baingan (Spinach-Aubergine)

This is a true blood Eastern India dish using *pachphoran*. You master this, and you can then cook any other *pachphoran* recipe with élan.

Serves 3-4

Ingredients

Spinach (*Palak*)–1 kg or 2lb or 4 cups (washed and chopped)

Aubergines (*Baingan*)-1 (roughly 200 grams or 7oz or 1 cup) (washed and cut into 1" cubes)

Onion Medium—1 (chopped)

Tomatoes—2 (washed and chopped)

Pachphoran, which is a mixture of *Jeera* (cumin), *Saunf* (fennel seeds), *Methi* seeds (fenugreek seeds), *Rai* (black mustard seeds), and *Kalonji* (onion seeds) in equal proportion–1 teaspoon

Cooking oil (preferably Mustard for the authentic Bengali taste)–1 tablespoon full

Salt-1/2 teaspoon (or to taste)

Method

Turn on the Instant Pot.

Press the sauté button, and add the oil.

As the oil heats up, add the *pachphoran*.

As the *pachphoran* begins to splutter (which takes a few seconds), add the chopped onions, and sauté for a minute.

Add the washed and chopped spinach, aubergine, and the tomatoes. Stir the same to mix it evenly. Switch off the sauté button.

Close the lid and press the vegetable button if there is one. Otherwise pressure cook for 2 minutes.

Release the pressure.

Now open the lid and again press the sauté button. This is because spinach gives out a lot of water. So, let it dry up somewhat before you serve.

At this juncture, add the salt and mix well.

That's all. Your delicious *Palak Baingan* is ready.

Prep time: 5 minutes

Cooking time: 10 minutes

Total time: 15 minutes

Note: Different Instant Pot models may have different designs or control options, so please feel free to adapt as you deem fit.

Mattar Paneer (Cottage Cheese with peas in a curry)

This is the classic North Indian dish that you will find everywhere, in homes, *dhabas,* as well as fancy restaurants. Here is a low-calorie version, however.

Serves 3-4

Ingredients

Paneer (Cottage cheese)–500 grams (approx. 18oz or 2 cups)

Green peas (shelled, fresh are preferred)–200 grams (approx. 7oz or 1 cup)

Medium-size Onions–2

Garlic-4 pieces

Ginger-1-inch (2.5 cm or 1/3rd length of a finger) piece

Fresh tomato-2 (washed and chopped)

Turmeric (*Haldi*) - 1/2 tea spoon

Dry crushed Coriander (*Dhania*) seeds-2 tea spoon

Garam Masala (mixture of common Indian spices) crushed- 1/2 tea spoon

Tip: If you can't get ready-made *garam masala* mixture from a nearby Indian store, you can make yours by using 1 black

cardamom, 3 green cardamoms, 4 cloves, and 1- inch cinnamon—all ground together for this dish.

Kashmiri Red Chilli powder–1/4 tea spoon (Recommended for color, but if you like your dish to be really spicy, use some other red chilli powder)

Cumin seeds whole (*Jeera*)-1/2 tea spoon

Salt-1 level tea spoon (or to taste)

Tomato Ketchup-1 table spoon

Cooking oil-1 table spoon

Ghee (clarified butter)-1 tea spoon

Water-1 tea cup

Method

Cut *paneer* into bite-size pieces.

Blend together (in a blender preferably!) the onions, garlic, ginger, and tomatoes to a fine paste.

Turn on the Instant Pot.

Press the sauté button, and take it to high.

Add the cooking oil in the inner pot.

When the oil warms up, add the cumin seeds, and as it turns brown, add the blended paste, and gently fry the same.

As the paste starts giving off a pleasant aroma, add the peas and the paneer and sauté gently.

Add all the dry *masala* and salt to this mixture.

Add the ketchup and *ghee* to the mixture and stir again.

Add the water, close the lid, and pressure cook for 2 minutes.

That's all. Your *Mattar paneer* (cottage cheese with peas curry) is ready.

Prep time: 5 minutes

Cooking time: 5 minutes

Total time: 10 minutes

Note: Different Instant Pot models may have different designs or control options, so please feel free to adapt as you deem fit.

Lauki Plain (Bottle Gourd)

This is the easiest way to cook *Lauki,* the Eastern Indian way, with absolutely the minimum of spices. So, no turmeric, no *garam masala*, or *pachphoran*. Nothing can be simpler and still be so tasty.

Serves 3-4

Ingredients

Lauki (Bottle Gourd)–1 (roughly a kg or 2lb or 4 cups); peel and cut into bite-size pieces

Onion Medium—1 (chopped)

Jeera (Cumin)–1/2 teaspoon

Dry Red Whole (not powder) Chilli–1 (Just for flavor and not to make the food spicy)

Salt–1 level teaspoon (or to taste)

Cooking oil–1 tablespoon

Method

Turn on the Instant Pot.

Press the sauté button.

In the inner pot, add the cooking oil and when it warms up, add the cumin seeds (*jeera*) and the dry red whole chilli.

As soon as the cumin (*jeera*) starts browning, add the chopped onion, and sauté it till these become translucent.

Add the *lauki* (bottle gourd) pieces, and the salt. Stir well.

Switch off the sauté button.

Close the lid, and press the vegetable button, if there be one. Otherwise pressure cook for 2 minutes.

Release the pressure.

Now open the lid and again press the sauté button.

This is because the bottle gourd (*lauki*) gives out a lot of water. So, let it dry up somewhat before you serve.

That's all. Your *Lauki Plain* is ready to be served.

Prep time: 5 minutes

Cooking time: 10 minutes

Total time: 15 minutes

Note: Different Instant Pot models may have different designs or control options, so please feel free to adapt as you deem fit.

Band Gobi, Gaajar, Aloo, Mattar ki Sabzi (Cabbage, Carrot, Potatoes, and Peas Curry)

This is a great medley of popular winter vegetables of India. You can, of course, follow this recipe to make your own medley of favorite veggies.

Serves 3-4

Ingredients

Cabbage–1/2 kg (500 grams or 18oz or 2 cups)

Green peas (shelled, fresh are preferred)–200 grams (7oz) (1 cup)

Potatoes-2 (chopped)

Carrots—2 (chopped)

Medium-size Onions–2 (chopped)

Garlic-4 cloves

Ginger-1-inch

Fresh tomatoes-2 (chopped)

Turmeric (*Haldi*) powder- 1/2 tea spoon

Dry crushed coriander (*Dhania*) powder-2 tea spoons

Garam Masala (mixture of common Indian spices) crushed- 1/2 tea spoon

Tip: If you can't get ready-made *garam masala* mixture from a nearby Indian store, you can make yours by using 1 black cardamom, 3 green cardamoms, 4 cloves, and 1- inch cinnamon—all ground together.

Kashmiri Red Chilli powder–1/4 tea spoon (Recommended for color, but if you like your dish to be really spicy, use some other hotter red chilli powder)

Cumin (*Jeera*) whole-1/2 tea spoon

Salt-1 level tea spoon (or to taste)

Tomato Ketchup-1 table spoon

Cooking oil-1 table spoon

Ghee (clarified butter)-1 tea spoon

Water-1 cup (200 ml)

Method

Blend together (in a blender preferably!) the onions, garlic, ginger, and tomatoes to a fine paste.

Cut cabbage, carrots, and potatoes somewhat roughly so that they retain their crunchiness even after they are cooked.

Turn on the Instant Pot.

Press the sauté button.

Now pour the oil in the inner pot.

As the oil heats up, add cumin seeds.

As these splutter and turn brown, add the paste from the blender, and gently fry it.

As the paste starts giving off a pleasant aroma, add all the vegetables (cabbage, carrot, peas, and potato) and sauté gently.

Add all the dry condiments and salt to this mixture and keep stirring till all the vegetables are well coated.

Add now the ketchup and *ghee* to the mixture and stir again.

Add the water.

Close the lid and press the vegetable button if there be one. Otherwise pressure cook for 2 minutes.

Release the pressure.

That's all. Your *band gobi, gaajar, aloo mattar sabzi* (cabbage, carrot, potatoes, and peas curry) is ready.

Prep time: 10 minutes

Cooking time: 7 minutes

Total time: 17 minutes

Note: Different Instant Pot models may have different designs or control options, so please feel free to adapt as you deem fit.

Aloo Gobi (Potato-Cauliflower)

This is a very popular North Indian dry veggie dish. Alone, it goes well with *pooris* (fried non leavened Indian bread). Otherwise, it can be paired with another curry dish and/or lentil dish and enjoyed with rice or *rotis*.

Serves 3-4

Ingredients

Potatoes-2

Cauliflower-1

Onion-1

Garlic-2

Ginger-1/2 inch

Turmeric (*Haldi*)-1/2 tea spoon

Garam Masala (mixture of common Indian spices) crushed- 1/2 tea spoon

Tip: If you can't get ready-made *garam masala* mixture from a nearby Indian store, you can make yours by using 1 black cardamom, 3 green cardamoms, 4 cloves, and 1- inch cinnamon—all ground together.

Kashmiri Red Chilli powder–1/4 tea spoon (Recommended for color, but if you like your dish to be really spicy, use some other hotter red chilli powder)

Tomato-1

Tomato Puree—1/2 cup (100 grams)

Salt-1 level tea spoon (or to taste)

Cooking Oil-2 table spoon

Water—1/2 cup

Method

Cut the potatoes into small pieces and also separate the florets of the cauliflower.

Next, chop the onion, garlic, ginger, and tomatoes and keep it separate.

Turn on the Instant Pot.

Press the sauté button.

Now pour the oil in the inner pot.

As the oil heats up, add the cauliflower florets and roast till these acquire a golden color.

Add the potatoes and stir well for a few minutes.

Now add the chopped onion, garlic, and ginger.

When this mixture starts becoming translucent, add the tomatoes, and let the tomatoes cook.

Sprinkle *haldi, garam masala, chilli powder, and salt* and stir for about three minutes.

Add the water and let it cook till all the water evaporates.

That's all. Your dry *aloo gobi* is ready.

Prep time: 10 minutes

Cooking time: 15 minutes

Total time: 25 minutes

Note: Different Instant Pot models may have different designs or control options, so please feel free to adapt as you deem fit.

Mixed Vegetables in Coconut Milk

If you want to be really adventurous, try making this South Indian mixed vegetable curry in coconut milk. Believe me, it tastes so heavenly that it will soon become your personal favorite.

This 6-vegetable medley with the goodness of coconut milk and so many Indian spices oozes health benefits from all its pores.

Serves 3-4

Ingredients

Yellow Pumpkin-150 grams (5oz) (half cup)

Carrot-100 grams (3.5oz) (half cup)

French Beans-100 grams (3.5oz) (half cup)

Cauliflower-100 grams (3.5oz) (half cup)

Potato-100 grams (3.5oz) (half cup)

Bottle Gourd-100 grams (3.5oz) (half cup)

Onion-1

Ginger-1-inch

Garlic-4 cloves

Tomato-1

(Onion+ Ginger+ Garlic + tomato- make into a fine paste in a blender)

Black Mustard (*Rai*) seeds-1/2 teaspoon

Curry leaves-a few

Coriander (*Dhania*) powder-2 teaspoon

Turmeric (*Haldi*) powder-1 teaspoon

Kashmiri Red Chilli powder–1/4 tea spoon (Recommended for color, but if you like your dish to be really spicy, use some other hotter red chilli powder)

Tamarind paste-1 tablespoon

Coconut milk-400 ml (1 + ½ cups)

Cooking oil-2 tablespoon

Salt- 1 level tea spoon (or to taste)

Method

Wash and cut the vegetables into bite-size pieces.

Prepare your onion + garlic+ ginger + tomato paste.

Turn on the Instant Pot.

Press the sauté button. Add the cooking oil in the inner pot.

When the oil warms, add the mustard seeds (*rai)* and the curry leaves.

When the rai splutters, add the onion + garlic+ ginger + tomato paste. Stir well.

Keep stirring till the paste is well fried and starts giving off a lovely aroma.

Note: Instead of making and frying the onion, garlic, ginger, and tomato paste, you can certainly use some ready-made fried paste, if you can manage to get that. This would save a lot of time as you don't have to first blend and then brown the onion + garlic+ ginger + tomato paste.

Add all the vegetables to this mixture and stir well.

Add the coriander, turmeric, red chilli powder, and the salt.

Keep stirring till all the vegetables are well coated.

Now, add a little water.

Close the lid and press the vegetable button if there is one. Otherwise pressure cook for 2 minutes.

Release the pressure.

Open the lid and now add the coconut milk and the tamarind paste.

Press the sauté button again and let the vegetables come to a boil.

That's all. Your mixed vegetables in coconut milk is ready to be served.

Prep time: 10 minutes

Cooking time: 7 minutes

Total time: 17 minutes

Note: Different Instant Pot models may have different designs or control options, so please feel free to adapt as you deem fit.

Green Peas and Potato Ghugni (Bihari style curry)

This is the favorite "Railway Station" dish all over North India that is usually served with *Pooris* (fried and puffed up unleavened Indian bread). A simple but finger-licking dish that everyone may fall in love with.

Serves 3-4

Ingredients

Green Peas- ½ cup (approx. 100 grams or 3.5 oz.)

Potato- 1 (cut into bite-size pieces)

Tomato- 2 (chopped)

Cumin seeds- ½ tea spoon

Cooking oil- 1 tea spoon

Water- 1/2 cup

Salt–1/2 tea spoon or to taste

Method

Turn on the Instant Pot.

Press the sauté button and take it to high.

Add the cooking oil in the inner pot.

When the oil warms up, add the cumin seeds.

As soon as the cumin seeds turn brown, which takes just a few seconds (do please make sure they don't burn), add the peas, and the potato.

Stir well for about a minute and add the tomatoes.

Stir till the tomatoes are slightly cooked.

Now add salt and the water.

Close the lid, and pressure cook for 5 minutes. Let it cool naturally.

That's all. Your Green Pea-Potato *Ghugni* is ready.

Prep time: 5 minutes

Cooking time: 5 minutes

Total time: 10 minutes

Note: Different Instant Pot models may have different designs or control options, so please feel free to adapt as you deem fit.

Meetha Kohra (Plain Pumpkin Delight-Sweet)

This Eastern Indian veggie is sweet, both literally and figuratively. Try this with *pooris* or *parathas,* and I'm sure you will agree that ripe pumpkin made any other way can't taste so delicious.

Serves 3-4

Ingredients

Ripe yellow pumpkin-1 kg (2lb) (4 cups)

Fenugreek seeds (*Methi*)-1/2 teaspoon

Coriander (*Dhania*) powder- 2 heap teaspoon

Turmeric (*Haldi*) powder-1 teaspoon

Kashmiri Red Chilli powder–1/2 tea spoon (Recommended for color, but if you like your dish to be really spicy, use some other hotter red chilli powder)

Mango Dry powder (*Amchoor*)-1/2 teaspoon

Asafoetida powder (*Hing*)-1 level teaspoon

Cooking Oil-2 tablespoon

Water-1 cup

Sugar-3 teaspoon

Salt-1 teaspoon (or to taste)

Method

Peel the pumpkin and cut into bite-size pieces.

Turn on the Instant Pot.

Press the sauté button.

In the inner pot, add the cooking oil.

When the cooking oil warms up, add the Fenugreek seeds (*Methi*), and thereafter add the pumpkins.

REMEMBER FENUGREEK SEEDS (METHI) BURN VERY FAST, SO DON'T LEAVE IT IN THE OIL WITHOUT THE PUMPKIN FOR MORE THAN A FEW SECONDS.

Now, add all the other ingredients.

Stir well for approximately 2 minutes to ensure that all the ingredients are well blended and very lightly fried.

Pour the water over the pumpkin.

Close the lid and press the vegetable button if there be one. Otherwise pressure cook for 2 minutes.

Release the pressure.

Open the lid and press the sauté button again.

Dry the pumpkin, that is, let the water evaporate till you have a nice thick consistency.

That's all. Your delicious *Meetha Kohra* pumpkin dish is ready.

Prep time: 10 minutes

Cooking time: 15 minutes

Total time: 25 minutes

Note: Different Instant Pot models may have different designs or control options, so please feel free to adapt as you deem fit.

Mushroom Mattar (Mushroom Peas Curry)

A very popular North Indian curry that most restaurants would be happy to serve in season.

Serves 3-4

Ingredients

Mushroom (e.g. white snow button)—500 grams (2 cup)-cut into 1/2

Green peas (shelled, fresh are preferred)–1/2 cup (100 grams or 3.5 oz.)

Medium-size Onions–2 (chopped)

Garlic-4 pieces

Ginger-1-inch (2.5 cm or 1/3rd length of a finger) piece

Fresh tomato-2 (chopped)

Turmeric (*Haldi*) - 1/2 tea spoon

Dry crushed coriander (*Dhania*) -2 tea spoon

Garam Masala (mixture of common Indian spices) crushed- 1/2 tea spoon

Tip: If you can't get ready-made *garam masala* mixture from a nearby Indian store, you can make yours by using 1 black

cardamom, 3 green cardamoms, 4 cloves, and 1- inch cinnamon—all ground together.

Kashmiri Red Chilli powder–1/4 tea spoon (Recommended for color, but if you like your dish to be really spicy, use any other red chilli powder)

Curd (Indian style plain yogurt)-1 table spoon

Cumin whole (*Jeera*)-1/2 tea spoon

Salt-1 level tea spoon (or to taste)

Tomato Ketchup-1 table spoon

Cooking oil-1 table spoon

Ghee (clarified butter)-1 tea spoon

Water-1 cup

Method

Blend together (in a blender preferably!) the onions, garlic, ginger, and tomatoes to a fine paste.

Turn on the Instant Pot.

Press the sauté button.

In the inner pot, heat the oil.

Add cumin to the oil and as it turns brown, add this paste, and gently fry the same.

As the paste starts giving off a pleasant aroma, add the mushroom and peas. Sauté gently.

Add all the dry condiments (*masala*), salt, and curd to this mixture and keep stirring till it starts becoming dry.

Add the ketchup to the mixture and stir again.

At this juncture, add the *ghee* for a lovely flavor.

Add the water.

Close the lid and press the vegetable button if there be one. Otherwise pressure cook for 2 minutes.

Let the Instant Pot cool on its own.

That's all. Your lovely Mushroom *Mattar* Curry is ready.

Prep time: 7 minutes

Cooking time: 10 minutes

Total time: 17 minutes

Note: Different Instant Pot models may have different designs or control options, so please feel free to adapt as you deem fit.

Paneer Makhni (Indian Cottage Cheese in a Rich Tomato Curry)

This is our vegetarian version of the popular Butter Chicken or the British Chicken Tikka Masala, except that we don't use any tandoor, *garam masala*, or even tear-jerking onions. The bright red curry is guaranteed to make this dish an instant hit with the young persons in your family.

Serves 3-4

Ingredients

Indian Cottage Cheese (*paneer*)–1/2 kg (500 grams or 18oz or 2 cups); cut into bite-size pieces

Chopped Tomatoes-3 large ripe

Tomato puree-200 grams (7oz) (1 cup)

Low fat fresh cream-200 grams (7oz) (1 cup)

Butter-1 tablespoon

Coriander (*Dhania*) powder-1 teaspoon

Cumin (*Jeera*) powder-1/2 teaspoon

Kashmiri Red Chilli powder–1/4 tea spoon (Recommended for color, but if you like your dish to be really spicy, use some other red chilli powder)

Salt-1 teaspoon or to taste

Sugar-1 teaspoon

Cooking Oil-2 tablespoon

Cashew nuts Chopped-50 grams (2oz or 3 tablespoon)

Method

Turn on the Instant Pot.

Press the sauté button.

In the inner pot, add the cooking oil and butter, and let it warm up.

When the butter melts, add the coriander, cumin, chopped cashew nuts, and the red chilli powder.

Let the mixture roast for 1 minute.

Add the tomatoes and cook till the tomatoes soften up.

Add the tomato puree, salt, and sugar.

Gently keep stirring.

As the gravy turns a nice thick red color, add the fresh low fat cream.

Stir well.

Now add the *paneer* pieces to the mixture and let it all come to a boil.

Let the mixture simmer for about 2 minutes.

Switch off the Instant Pot.

That's all. Your delicious *Paneer Makhni* is ready.

Prep time: 7 minutes

Cooking time: 10 minutes

Total time: 17 minutes

Note: Different Instant Pot models may have different designs or control options, so please feel free to adapt as you deem fit.

Aloo Bharta (Mashed Potato)

This typically Eastern India, or rather Bihari, dish is a must with Khichdi. I give a milder version here. But if you need to spice it up, then mix some stuffed red chilli pickles (or any other Indian pickles of your choice) to this and enjoy.

Serves 3-4

Ingredients

Potatoes-1/2 kg (18oz) (2 cups)

Onion-1 (chopped finely)

Green chilli de-seeded (for flavor)-1 (Use the seeds if you like it hot!)

Fresh Coriander (*Dhania*) leaves-50 grams (2oz) (3 tablespoon)

Mustard oil (if you want the authentic flavor; otherwise your preferred cooking oil)-1/2 teaspoon

Salt-to taste

Method

Turn on the Instant Pot.

In the inner pot, place the potatoes with enough water to cover them.

Close the lid and press the vegetable button, if there be one. Otherwise, pressure cook for 5 minutes.

Let the Instant Pot cool on its own.

Remove the potatoes, peel, and mash them well in a separate bowl.

Add the salt and the mustard oil.

Add the onion, chillies, and coriander (all raw).

Mix well.

That's all. Your *Bihari Aloo Bharta* is ready.

Prep time: Approx. 15 minutes.

Only the time taken to boil and peel the potatoes and to chop onions, etc.

Cooking time: No cooking time

Total time: 15 minutes maximum

Note: Different Instant Pot models may have different designs or control options, so please feel free to adapt as you deem fit.

Paneer Kaju Curry (Indian Cottage Cheese with Cashew and Black Pepper)

This is a "white curry" dish, with NO chillies of any kind, which the young persons in your family may find just irresistible.

Serves 3-4

Ingredients

Indian Cottage Cheese (*paneer*)–1/2 kg (500 grams or 18oz or 2 cups); cut into bite-size pieces

Low fat fresh cream-400 grams (14oz) (2 cup)

Butter-1 tablespoon

Salt- ½ teaspoon or to taste

Sugar- ½ teaspoon

Cashew nuts- 1 cup (crushed)

Black Pepper- 1 tablespoon (crushed)

Cooking Oil–2 tablespoon

Method

Turn on the Instant Pot.

Press the sauté button.

Add the cooking oil in the inner pot and let it warm up.

Now add the cottage cheese (*paneer*) pieces, and gently roast till they become golden.

Remove the *paneer* pieces and keep aside.

Now add the butter to the inner pot.

When the butter melts, add the crushed cashew nuts, and roast for about two minutes.

Now add the fresh cream, salt, and sugar, and bring the mixture to a boil while stirring continuously.

Add the roasted *paneer* pieces and let the mixture again come to a boil.

Let the mixture simmer for about 2 minutes.

Sprinkle the crushed black pepper.

Switch off the Instant Pot.

That's all. Your delicious *Paneer Kaju* Curry is ready.

Prep time: 7 minutes

Cooking time: 10 minutes

Total time: 17 minutes

Note: Different Instant Pot models may have different designs or control options, so please feel free to adapt as you deem fit.

Chapter 7: Fish Recipes

*"They say fish should swim thrice * * * first it should swim in the sea (do you mind me?) then it should swim in butter, and at last, sirrah, it should swim in good claret."*

Jonathan Swift

"Give a man a fish and he will ask for tartar sauce and French fries! Moreover, some politician who wants his vote will declare all these things to be among his 'basic rights.'"

Thomas Sowell

If you think, like Jonathan Swift above, that fish needs to be cooked only with butter and wine, or like Thomas Sowell that the tastiest way to have fish is with tartar sauce and French fries, then you need to think again.

While there definitely are some fishing communities which love sun-dried, stinky fish, most Asian traditions of cooking fish employ a number of flavorful techniques to mask whatever little "smell" the fish may have acquired in its journey from the sea, river, or lake to your plate.

This in the Thai tradition could mean the use of galangal, kafir lime leaves, and lemongrass. The Chinese would, of course, be liberal with their soya sauce, chilli sauce, and fish oil. The Japanese would often be so frugal with their spicing that they would leave their fish almost raw. But they would compensate that with the most exquisitely carved sushi rolls that your mind can ever conjure.

But the Indians use nothing that the Chinese, Japanese, Thai, or the Koreans are so fond of. Instead they seem to dunk their fish in almost everything that grows in their backyards and still manage to come up with so many flavorful preparations.

So, if you were wondering how to incorporate this superb, dripping with long strands of polyunsaturated essential omega-3 fatty acids (that the human body can't naturally produce), low-calorie, high quality, protein rich, white meat in your daily diet, just join us on this roller coaster journey of mindboggling seasoning and spices which only the Indians can manage.

This chapter is a humble attempt to sample 5 such mouth-watering "Home-Style" ways to cooking fish in a JIFFY as only Indians Can.

For more fish recipes, please feel free to refer to my book "The Ultimate Guide to Cooking Fish the Indian Way" that has 43 such recipes.

Machher Jhol (Fish Cooked in a Light Curry)

A simple fish curry from Eastern India that is eaten almost daily in many homes in West Bengal. This recipe uses a bit of *garam masala* but no *pachphoran* (a mixture of five spices) that most other fish dishes from Bengal use.

Serves 3-4

Ingredients

Sliced Fish —1/2 kg (18oz) (2 cups)

Note: If frozen, please thaw the fish first.

Tomatoes -2 (make into a paste)

Onion-1 small (chopped)

Garlic-2 pieces

Ginger-1-inch

(Onion+ Garlic + Ginger- make into a paste in a blender)

Salt—1 teaspoon (or to taste)

Sugar—1/4 teaspoon

Coriander (*Dhania*) powder—1 teaspoon

Garam Masala- 1/2 teaspoon

Tip: If you can't get ready-made *garam masala* mixture from a nearby Indian store, you can make yours by using 1 black cardamom, 3 green cardamoms, 4 cloves, and 1- inch cinnamon—all ground together for this dish.

Turmeric (*Haldi*)—1 and 1/2 teaspoon (1 teaspoon for marinating the fish and half for the curry).

Red Chilli powder— 1/4 teaspoon (just for flavor and not to make it hot; you can add more if you like it hot)

Fresh green chillies whole—4 (Whole chillies only impart a lovely flavor to the cuisine and will NOT make it spicy)

Mustard oil—3 tablespoon (If you want that classic taste, otherwise use whatever oil you normally use for frying)

Cumin seeds (*Jeera*)-1 teaspoon

Water-1 cup (roughly 300 ml)

Method

Sprinkle 1/2 teaspoon of salt and 1 teaspoon of the turmeric on the fish (cleaned and washed) to coat it on all sides.

Switch on the Instant Pot and press the sauté button.

Heat 2 tablespoon of oil (the third tablespoon to be used for making the curry) in the inner pot and gently fry the fish @ only 2-3 pieces of fish at a time.

After the fish turns a nice golden brown, remove to a plate, and add the next batch to the oil.

Please ensure that the fish does not burn.

When all the fish is fried and kept aside, add the third tablespoon of oil.

As the oil heats up, add the cumin seeds, and let it brown.

Do please make sure that it does not burn.

Add onion+ garlic + ginger paste and stir well.

Add the salt, turmeric powder, coriander powder, red chilli powder, *garam masala*, and sugar.

Keep on stirring till the paste is fried and you can see the oil glistening on the sides of the wok.

Add the tomato paste and stir well till the tomato is cooked.

Add 1 cup of water.

Add the fried fish to this mixture and also add the whole fresh green chillies.

When the mixture comes to a boil, cook it for 2 more minutes.

Switch off the Instant Pot.

That's all. Your classic *Machher Jhol* (Fish Cooked in a Light Curry) is ready.

Prep time: 5 minutes

Cooking time: 10 minutes

Total time: 15 minutes

Note: Different Instant Pot models may have different designs or control options, so please feel free to adapt as you deem fit.

Fish in Creamy Tomato Curry

Inspired by the famous Butter Chicken or the British Tikka Masala recipe, the bright red curry with its mellow taste will make this dish an instant hit with the young persons in your family.

Serves 3-4

Ingredients

Boneless Fish filet-1/2 kg (18oz) (2 cups); cut into serving-size pieces

Note: If frozen, please thaw the fish first.

For the marinade:

Plain Yogurt-2 tablespoon

Chopped Ginger-1-inch piece

Chopped Garlic-6 cloves

Coriander (*Dhania*) powder-1 teaspoon

Red chilli powder-1/4 teaspoon (just for flavor and not to make it hot; you can add more if you like it hot)

Cumin (*Jeera*) powder-1/2 teaspoon

Salt- 1/2 teaspoon or to taste

Cooking oil- 1 tablespoon

For the gravy:

Chopped Tomatoes-3 large ripe

Tomato puree-200 grams (1 cup)

Low fat fresh cream-200 grams (1 cup)

Butter-1 tablespoon

Coriander (*Dhania*) powder-1 teaspoon

Cumin (*Jeera*) powder-1/2 teaspoon

Red chilli powder-1/4 teaspoon (just for flavor and not to make it hot; you can add more if you like it hot)

Salt- 1 teaspoon or to taste

Sugar-1 teaspoon or to taste

Method

Make the fish

Marinate the fish (cleaned and washed) for about 10 minutes in all the ingredients mentioned for the marinade, except the oil.

Switch on the Instant Pot and press the sauté button.

Add a tablespoon of cooking oil in the inner pot.

When the oil heats up, add the fish with the marinade, and cook lightly.

Don't stir with a spatula as you may break the fish, but you can use it to flip the fish once carefully.

Switch off the sauté button.

Remove the fish from the inner pot and keep it aside in a plate.

Make the gravy

In the inner pot, now add the butter.

Press the sauté button again.

When the butter melts, add the coriander, cumin, and the chilli powder.

Let the mixture roast for 1 minute.

Add the tomatoes, and cook till the tomatoes soften up.

Add the tomato puree and the salt and sugar.

Gently keep stirring.

As the gravy turns a nice thick red color, add the low fat fresh cream. Stir well.

Add the fish in the gravy and let it simmer for about 2 minutes.

Switch off the Instant Pot.

That's all. Your delicious Fish in a Creamy Tomato Curry is ready.

Prep time: 15 minutes (including marinating time)

Cooking time: 15 minutes

Total time: 30 minutes

Note: Different Instant Pot models may have different designs or control options, so please feel free to adapt as you deem fit.

Machhi Do Pyaza (Fish with fried onions)

Again a popular North Indian dish that goes well with *Rotis*, the Indian unleavened bread.

Serves 3-4

Ingredients

Sliced Fish —1/2 kg (18oz) (2 cups)

Note: If frozen, please thaw the fish first.

Onion-1 large (chopped)

Ginger-2-inch piece

Garlic-8 Cloves

Tomatoes-3 (chopped)

(Onion + Ginger + Garlic + Tomatoes blended and made into a fine paste)

Onions- 2 large (chopped) separately for frying

Salt—1 teaspoon (or to taste)

Turmeric (*Haldi*)—1 and 1/2 teaspoon (1 teaspoon for marinating the fish and half for the curry).

Red Chilli powder— 1/4 teaspoon (just for flavor and not to make it hot; you can add more if you like it hot)

Fresh green chillies whole—4 (Whole chillies only impart a lovely flavor to the cuisine and will NOT make it spicy)

Mustard oil—4 tablespoon (If you want that classic taste, otherwise whatever oil you normally use)

Water-1/2 cup (roughly 125 ml)

Method

Sprinkle 1/2 teaspoon of salt and 1 teaspoon of the turmeric on the fish (cleaned and washed) to coat it on all sides.

Switch on the Instant Pot and press the sauté button.

Heat 3 tablespoon of oil (the fourth tablespoon to be used for making the curry) in the inner pot and gently fry the fish @ only 2-3 pieces of fish at a time.

After the fish turns a nice golden brown, remove to a plate, and add the next batch to the oil.

Please ensure that the fish does not burn.

When all the fish is fried and kept aside, add the fourth tablespoon of fresh oil to the pot.

As the oil heats up, add the chopped onions, and fry till it turns golden.

Remove the onion from the Instant Pot and keep aside.

Now put the onion+ garlic + ginger+ tomato paste in the inner pot and stir well.

Add the salt, remaining turmeric powder, and the red chilli powder.

Keep on stirring till the paste is fried and you can see the oil glistening on the sides of the inner pot.

Add ½ cup of water.

Now add the fried fish to this mixture and also add the whole fresh green chillies and the fried onions.

When the mixture comes to a boil, cook for 2 more minutes.

That's all. Your *Machhi Do Pyaza* (Fish with fried onions) is ready.

Prep time: 10 minutes

Cooking time: 10 minutes

Total time: 20 minutes

Note: Different Instant Pot models may have different designs or control options, so please feel free to adapt as you deem fit.

Dahi Sarson Machhali (Fish cooked in a Yogurt and Mustard paste)

Our tribute to yet another timeless fish preparation from West Bengal. This dish neither uses *garam masala* nor *pachphoran* and yet is unusually tasty.

Serves 3-4

Ingredients

Sliced Fish —1/2 kg (18oz) (2 cups)

Note: If frozen, please thaw the fish first.

Plain Yogurt—400 grams (14oz or 1 + 1/2 cups)

Mustard paste—4 tablespoon (*Kasundi*-ready-made paste is preferred; or just use English mustard paste)

Milk—1/2 cup

Salt—1 and 1/2 teaspoon (or to taste)

Sugar—1 teaspoon

Fresh green chillies whole—4 (Whole chillies only impart a lovely flavor to the cuisine and will NOT make it spicy)

Mustard oil (or your preferred cooking oil)—1 teaspoon

Turmeric (*Haldi*)—1 teaspoon

Chickpea flour (*Besan*)—1 teaspoon

Method

In the inner pot, beat up the yogurt, mustard paste, milk, chickpea flour, salt, and sugar to a smooth blend WITHOUT switching on the Instant Pot.

Add the raw mustard oil to this mixture.

Add the fish to this mixture and also add the whole fresh green chillies.

Now, switch on the Instant Pot and press the sauté button.

When the mixture comes to a boil, let it boil for 5 minutes. Keep stirring gently so as not to break the fish and to ensure that the yogurt does not split.

That's all. Your *Dahi Sarson* Fish (Fish cooked in a Yogurt and Mustard paste) is ready.

Prep time: 5 minutes

Cooking time: 5 minutes

Total time: 10 minutes

Note: Different Instant Pot models may have different designs or control options, so please feel free to adapt as you deem fit.

Meen Moily (Fish Kerala style)

This is our tribute to the robust fish eating tradition of Kerala, the southernmost state of India. This dish bristles with the goodness of coconut milk and coconut powder. The typical "South Indian" taste comes from *Rai* (black mustard seeds) and curry leaves.

Serves 3-4

Ingredients

Fish-1/2 kg (18oz) (2 cups) cut into pieces

Note: If frozen, please thaw the fish first.

Chopped Onion-1

Chopped Ginger-2 inch

Coconut Milk-200 ml (1 cup approximately)

Coconut powder-2 tablespoon (dissolved in ¼ cup water).

Lemon juice-1

Rai (Black mustard seeds) -1/2 teaspoon

Curry leaves-few

Salt—1 teaspoon (or to taste)

Cooking Oil -1 tablespoon (Use a milder flavored oil such as groundnut, sesame, or coconut for the best effect)

Method

Sprinkle a little salt on the fish pieces (cleaned and washed).

Switch on the Instant Pot and press the sauté button. Add the oil in the inner pot, and when it heats up, add the mustard seeds until they crackle.

Immediately add the chopped onion and ginger and stir well.

Sauté for a few minutes and add the curry leaves.

Add the coconut milk and the coconut powder (dissolve the powder in ¼ cup of water beforehand).

Add the fish and rest of the salt.

Let the mixture come to a boil. Cook for 2 minutes.

Switch off the sauté button.

Add the lemon juice.

That's all. Your *Meen Moily* (Fish Kerala style) is ready.

This dish goes really well with plain boiled rice.

Prep time: 5 minutes

Cooking time: 10 minutes

Total time: 15 minutes

Note: Different Instant Pot models may have different designs or control options, so please feel free to adapt as you deem fit.

Prawn Malai Curry (Prawns in a mild coconut and cream curry)

This mild but delicious curry is from the Eastern state of West Bengal. Try it once and the younger persons of your family will be hooked on forever.

Serves 3-4

Ingredients

Prawns de-veined-500 grams (18oz) (roughly 2 cups)

Note: If frozen, please thaw the prawns first.

(Only de-shell the top portion but let the head remain attached to the shell. This adds a lot of flavor and taste to the curry)

Onion-1 (chopped)

Garlic-4 cloves (large)

Ginger-1-inch

(Onion+ Garlic + Ginger- make into a paste in a blender)

Garam Masala-1/2 teaspoon

Tip: If you can't get ready-made *garam masala* mixture from a nearby Indian store, you can make yours by using 1 black cardamom, 3 green cardamoms, 4 cloves, and 1-inch cinnamon—all ground together for this dish.

Red Chilli Powder-1/4 teaspoon (just for flavor and not to make it hot; you can add more if you like it hot)

Cumin Seeds (*Jeera*)-1 teaspoon

Ghee (Clarified butter)-1 tablespoon

Coconut milk-200 ml (1 cup)

Low fat cream-200 ml (1 cup)

Green Chillies Whole-2 (for flavor)

Salt- 1 teaspoon or to taste

Method

Switch on the Instant Pot and press the sauté button. Add the *ghee* and when it warms up, add the cumin seeds.

The moment the cumin seeds start browning, add the (Onion + Garlic + Ginger) paste.

Gently stir the mixture and as the mixture starts to brown, add the *garam masala*, red chilli powder and salt (to taste) for the curry.

When the oil separates, add the coconut milk and the low fat cream, and mix well.

Add the prawns and the whole green chillies and let the whole mixture come to a boil. Cook for 2 minutes.

Remove from fire.

That's all. Your *Malai* Prawn Curry is ready.

Prep Time: 5 minutes

Cooking Time: 10 minutes

Total Time: 15 minutes

Note: Different Instant Pot models may have different designs or control options, so please feel free to adapt as you deem fit.

Chapter 8: Chicken, Egg, and Mutton Recipes

Anyone interacting with the peripatetic Indian businessmen, who hail predominantly from the western Indian states of Gujarat or Rajasthan, may think Indians to be primarily vegetarian. Once in India, they are then justifiably shocked to find a flourishing omnivorous tradition.

Some attribute this to the influence of rulers who came from Turkey, Persia, or any of the Central Asian States like Uzbekistan. This is evident from the very popular body of dishes that goes around the banner of *Mughlai* cuisine.

Certainly much of the baking tradition, especially using tandoors (earthen ovens) would have come from these regions. But barbeque, I'm not so sure that it is not as ancient as the discovery of fire and roasting of the hunt-of-the-day thereon.

And what would you say to the South Indian and, in fact, the entire Coastal Indian tradition of cooking their meats and fishes with coconut, curry leaves, and *Rai* (black mustard seeds)? And the Eastern Indian tradition of using *Pachphoran*? Original and quite unparalleled? Yes absolutely, because no West Asian or East Asian nation cooks like the South, West, and East Indians do.

That leaves the North Indian cuisine which prima facie looks "influenced." I've, however, scoured the lanes of Samarkand and Bukhara for any *Mughlai* dish and failed. I couldn't even get a simple curry anywhere. There was no trace of *Dal Bukhara* (or any lentil dish) even in the priciest of restaurants in Bukhara. Yes, I could have Rice *Pilaf*, but they were sweet and made in cotton seed oil. These tasted so different from any Indian *Pulao or Biryani* that I am not sure whether the Central Asians inspired us or whether we taught them a trick or two. The kebabs contained NO spices. The desserts didn't use milk or milk products. I could go on and on ...

Made me wonder if we are being too self-deprecatory and too generous in giving credit to "foreign" influences?

Before I spark off a major controversy, let me stop here and focus on the "Home Style" non-vegetarian dishes of my home.

In that background, I present seven chicken, six mutton, and one egg recipe spanning the Northern, Eastern, and Southern Indian traditions. You master this and you can handle any Indian non-vegetarian dish, I promise.

For more chicken recipes, please feel free to refer to my book "The Ultimate Guide to Cooking Chicken the Indian Way" that has 51 such recipes.

Basic Indian Chicken Curry

This is the Basic Indian Chicken Curry that once mastered can be easily adapted into a number of variations simply by adding or deleting some ingredients. It is the East Indian version from the states of Bihar and Bengal that we present here.

Serves 3-4

Ingredients

Whole chicken -1 approx. 800 grams or 28oz (4 cups) (cut into 8 pieces)

Chopped Onions-3 large

Chopped Ginger-2-inch piece

Chopped Garlic-8 Cloves

Chopped Tomatoes-3

Coriander (*Dhania*) powder-2 teaspoon

Turmeric powder (*Haldi*)-1 teaspoon

Garam Masala-1 teaspoon

Tip: If you can't get ready-made *garam masala* mixture from a nearby Indian store, you can make yours by using 1 black cardamom, 3 green cardamoms, 4 cloves, and 1- inch cinnamon—all ground together for this dish.

Red Chilli powder-1/4 teaspoon (just for flavor and not to make it hot; you can add more if you like it hot)

Cumin seeds (*Jeera*)-1/2 teaspoon

Tomato Ketchup-2 tablespoon

Cooking Oil-2 tablespoon

Ghee (Clarified butter)-1 tablespoon

Water-3 cups

Salt- 1 teaspoon or to taste

Method

Switch on the Instant Pot and press the sauté button.

Add the oil in the inner pot.

As the oil turns hot, add the cumin seeds, and let them splutter.

Immediately add the chopped onion.

Stir well till the onions become translucent.

Now, add the chopped ginger and garlic, and stir till it all starts giving off a pleasant aroma.

Add the chicken pieces and the *ghee* (clarified butter).

Stir well.

Add the coriander powder, turmeric, *garam masala*, and red chilli powder.

Stir and cook the chicken till all the water evaporates, and the chicken becomes almost dry. This process ensures that all the raw flavors of chicken, onions, etc. are removed.

Add now the tomatoes and the ketchup.

Stir well again and add the salt.

Let the tomatoes cook well.

Now, add the water, and switch off the sauté button. Close the lid of the inner pot, and press the chicken button, if there be one. Otherwise, pressure cook for 10 minutes.

Let the Instant Pot cool down on its own.

That's all. Your basic Indian Chicken Curry is now ready.

Prep time: 7 minutes

Cooking time: 10 minutes

Total time: 17 minutes

Note: Different Instant Pot models may have different designs or control options, so please feel free to adapt as you deem fit.

Thick Chicken Curry

This is a tastier twist on the Basic Indian Chicken Curry that is quite popular in the East Indian states of Bihar and Bengal. The "twist" comes from the addition of eggs and potatoes.

Serves 3-4

Ingredients

Whole chicken -1 approx. 800 grams or 28oz (4 cups) (cut into 8 pieces)

Onions-3 large (chopped)

Ginger-2-inch piece

Garlic-8 Cloves

Tomatoes-3 (chopped)

(Onion + Ginger + Garlic + Tomatoes blended and made into a fine paste)

Coriander powder-2 teaspoon

Turmeric (*Haldi*)-1 teaspoon

Garam Masala-1 teaspoon

Tip: If you can't get ready-made *garam masala* mixture from a nearby. Indian store, you can make yours by using 1 black cardamom, 3 green cardamoms, 4 cloves, and 1- inch cinnamon—all ground together for this dish.

Red Chilli powder-1/4 teaspoon (just for flavor and not to make it hot; you can add more if you like it hot)

Cumin seeds (Jeera)-1/2 teaspoon

Potatoes-2 (peeled and cut into big pieces)

Cooking Oil-3 tablespoon

Ghee (Clarified butter)-1 tablespoon

Water-3 cups

Egg-1

Sugar-1/2 teaspoon

Salt- 1 teaspoon or to taste

Method

Switch on the Instant Pot and press the sauté button.

Add the oil in the inner pot.

As the oil turns hot, add the cumin seeds, and let them splutter.

Immediately add the Onion + Ginger + Garlic + Tomatoes fine paste.

Stir well till the paste starts giving off a pleasant aroma, and you can see the oil ooze out from the sides.

Add the chicken and stir well.

Add the coriander, turmeric, *garam masala*, and the red chilli powder.

Cook the chicken till all the water evaporates, and the chicken becomes somewhat dry.

Add the potatoes.

Stir well again and add salt and the sugar.

Now, add the water, and switch off the sauté button. Close the lid of the inner pot, and press the chicken button, if there be one. Otherwise, pressure cook for 10 minutes.

Let the Instant Pot cool down on its own.

Open the Instant Pot and press the sauté button again.

Meanwhile, beat up the egg in a bowl.

As the curry comes to a boil, gently add the egg stirring continuously.

Switch off the Instant Pot.

That's all. Your Thick Chicken Curry is ready.

Prep time: 10 minutes

Cooking time: 15 minutes

Total time: 25 minutes

Note: Different Instant Pot models may have different designs or control options, so please feel free to adapt as you deem fit.

Chicken Korma (Chicken in a Mughlai White Curry)

This is a classic preparation from North India that claims its heritage from the days of the Grand Mughals. The dish uses NO chillies, red or green, and so can be served to people of all ages who would love this somewhat "safer" introduction to Indian cuisine.

Serves 3-4

Ingredients

Chicken pieces-1 kg (2 lbs) (4 cups)

Onions chopped finely-500 grams (18oz) (2 cups)

Garlic chopped-8 cloves

Ginger chopped-2-inch piece

Green Cardamom (*Chhoti Elaichi*)-4

Brown Cardamom (*Badi Elaichi*)-2

Cinnamon (*Dalchinni*)-1-inch stick

Cloves (*Laung*)-6

Bay Leaves (*Tejpatta*)-2

Cumin Seeds (*Jeera*)-1 teaspoon

Cashew nuts-3 tablespoon

Blanched Almonds-3 tablespoon

(To blanch almonds, immerse them in half a cup of hot water for 30 minutes. Remove the skin thereafter.)

Raisins-3 tablespoon

(Cashew nuts + Almonds + Raisins to be blended into a fine paste)

Desiccated coconut-2 tablespoon

Fresh dairy cream-1/2 cup

Yogurt unsweetened (Indian set curd is preferred)-200 grams (8oz) 1 cup

Cooking Oil-2 tablespoon

Clarified Butter (*ghee*)-2 tablespoon

Salt- 1 teaspoon or to taste

Water-2 cups

Method

Switch on the Instant Pot and press the sauté button.

Add the cooking oil and the *ghee* together in the inner pot.

As soon as the oil heats up, add the cardamom, bay leaves, cinnamon, cloves, and the cumin seeds. Let them brown for a few seconds.

Add the onions, and roast till the onions become translucent. Add the garlic and ginger and let them roast for a few minutes.

Add the chicken pieces and fry well.

Now add the dry fruits (Cashew nuts + Almonds + Raisins) paste and again roast.

Add the desiccated coconut and yogurt.

Stir till all the water has evaporated. Now add the salt and water. Switch off the sauté button.

Close the lid of the inner pot and press the chicken button, if there be one. Otherwise, pressure cook for 10 minutes.

Let the Instant Pot cool down on its own.

After opening the Instant Pot, add the fresh cream.

That's all. Your delicious Chicken Korma is ready.

Prep time: 10 minutes

Cooking time: 20 minutes

Total time: 30 minutes

Note: Different Instant Pot models may have different designs or control options, so please feel free to adapt as you deem fit.

Chicken Keema Mattar (Chicken Mince Peas Curry)

This is yet another dish that infuses the goodness of legumes into your chicken and helps you attain nutritional Nirvana in a JIFFY.

Serves 3-4

Ingredients

Chicken mince—1/2 kg (500 grams or 18oz or 2 cups)

Green peas (shelled, fresh are preferred) —200 grams (7oz) (1 cup)

Medium-size Onions—2 (chopped)

Garlic-4 pieces

Ginger-1-inch

Fresh tomato-2 (chopped)

Turmeric (*Haldi*) - 1/2 teaspoon

Dry crushed coriander (*Dhania*)-2 teaspoon

Garam Masala (mixture of common Indian spices) crushed- 1/2 teaspoon

Tip: If you can't get ready-made *garam masala* mixture from a nearby Indian store, you can make yours by using 1 black

cardamom, 3 green cardamoms, 4 cloves, and 1- inch cinnamon—all ground together for this dish.

Kashmiri Red Chilli powder—1/4 tea spoon (Recommended for color, but if you like your dish to be really spicy, use any other red chilli powder)

Yogurt unsweetened (Indian set curd is preferred)-1 tablespoon

Cumin whole (*Jeera*)-1/2 teaspoon

Salt-1/2 teaspoon (or to taste)

Tomato Ketchup-1 tablespoon

Cooking oil-1 tablespoon

Ghee (clarified butter)-1 teaspoon

Water-1 tea cup

Method

Blend together (in a blender preferably!) the onions, garlic, ginger, and tomatoes to a fine paste.

Switch on the Instant Pot and press the sauté button.

Heat the oil in the inner pot.

Add cumin seeds to the oil, and as they turn brown, add the paste from the blender and gently fry.

As the paste starts giving off a pleasant aroma, add the chicken mince, and sauté gently.

Add the *garam masala*, turmeric, crushed coriander, red chilli powder, salt, and curd to this mixture, and keep stirring till they start becoming almost dry.

Add the ketchup and peas to the mixture and stir again.

At this juncture, add the *ghee* for a lovely taste.

Now, add the water, and switch off the sauté button.

Close the lid of the inner pot and press the chicken button, if there be one. Otherwise, pressure cook for 5 minutes.

Let the Instant Pot cool down on its own.

That's all. Your Chicken *Keema Mattar* is ready.

Prep time: 7 minutes

Cooking time: 10 minutes

Total time: 17 minutes

Note: Different Instant Pot models may have different designs or control options, so please feel free to adapt as you deem fit.

Chicken in a Coconut Curry

This is a South Indian style chicken recipe. If you have had only North Indian style chicken so far, try this finger-licking dish with such exotic flavors that they are sure to wow you over.

Serves 3-4

Ingredients

Whole chicken -1 approx. 800 grams or 28oz or 4 cups (cut into 8 pieces)

Onion-1 large (chopped)

Ginger-1-inch piece

Garlic-6 Cloves

Tomatoes-2 (chopped)

(Onion + Ginger + Garlic + Tomatoes blended and made into a fine paste)

Coriander (*Dhania*) powder-2 teaspoon

Turmeric (*Haldi*) powder-1 teaspoon

Garam Masala-1 teaspoon

Tip: If you can't get ready-made *garam masala* mixture from a nearby Indian store, you can make yours by using 1 black cardamom, 3 green cardamoms, 4 cloves, and 1- inch cinnamon—all ground together for this dish.

Red Chilli powder-1/4 teaspoon (just for flavor and not to make it hot; you can add more if you like it hot)

Black Mustard seeds (*Rai*)-1/2 teaspoon

Curry leaves- 10-12

Coconut Milk-400 ml (1 + ½ cups)

Potatoes-2 (peeled and cut into small pieces)

Cooking Oil-3 tablespoon

Salt- 1 teaspoon or to taste

Method

Switch on the Instant Pot and press the sauté button.

Add the oil in the inner pot.

As the oil turns hot, add the black mustard seeds, and let them splutter.

Immediately add the Onion + Ginger + Garlic + Tomatoes fine paste.

Add the curry leaves, and stir well till the paste starts giving off a pleasant aroma, and you can see the oil ooze out from the sides.

Add the chicken pieces and stir well.

Add the coriander, turmeric, *garam masala*, and red chilli powder.

Cook the chicken till all the water evaporates, and the chicken is somewhat dry.

Add the potatoes. Stir well again.

Now add the coconut milk and salt.

Switch off the sauté button. Close the lid of the inner pot, and press the chicken button, if there be one. Otherwise, pressure cook for 10 minutes.

Let the Instant Pot cool down on its own.

That's all. Your Chicken in Coconut Milk is ready.

Prep time: 10 minutes

Cooking time: 15 minutes

Total time: 25 minutes

Note: Different Instant Pot models may have different designs or control options, so please feel free to adapt as you deem fit.

Murg Badami (Chicken Almond Curry)

This is a gourmet dish that you may rarely find even in a 5-star restaurant in India. Attempt this, therefore, only in a somewhat relaxed frame of mind. Almonds and saffron make this a very different (and somewhat expensive) dish.

Serves 3-4

Ingredients

Whole chicken -1 approx. 800 grams or 28oz or 4 cups (cut into 8 pieces)

Chopped Onions-3 large

Sliced Onions- 2 large

Chopped Ginger-2-inch piece

Chopped Garlic-8 Cloves

Chopped Tomatoes-3

Coriander (*Dhania*) powder-2 teaspoon

Turmeric (*Haldi*) powder-1 teaspoon

Fennel (*Saunf*) - ½ teaspoon (ground)

Poppy seeds (*Khaskhas*) - 1 teaspoon (ground)

Garam Masala-1 teaspoon

Tip: If you can't get ready-made *garam masala* mixture from a nearby Indian store, you can make yours by using 1 black cardamom, 3 green cardamoms, 4 cloves, and 1-inch cinnamon—all ground together for this dish.

Red Chilli powder-1/4 teaspoon (just for flavor and not to make it hot; you can add more if you like it hot)

Cumin (*Jeera*) seeds-1/2 teaspoon

Saffron (*Kesar*) strands- ½ teaspoon (dissolved in two tablespoon hot water)

Tomato Ketchup-2 tablespoon

Yogurt unsweetened (Indian set curd is preferred)-200 grams (8oz) or 1 cup (water drained)

Almonds- ½ cup (blanched)

(To blanch almonds, immerse them in half a cup of hot water for 30 minutes. Remove the skin thereafter.)

Cooking Oil-2 tablespoon

Ghee (Clarified butter)-1 tablespoon

Water-2 cups

Salt- 1 and ½ teaspoon or to taste

Method

Switch on the Instant Pot and press the sauté button.

Heat the oil and *ghee* together in the inner pot and fry the two sliced onions till they turn golden brown.

Take out the onions and keep aside.

As the oil/*ghee* would still be hot, add the cumin seeds and let them splutter.

Immediately add the three chopped onions.

Stir well till the onions become translucent.

Now, add the chopped ginger and garlic and stir till these start giving off a pleasant aroma.

Add the chicken pieces.

Stir well.

Add the coriander powder, turmeric powder, fennel powder, *garam masala*, and red chilli powder.

Stir and cook the chicken till all the water evaporates, and the chicken becomes almost dry. This process ensures that all the raw flavors of chicken, onions, etc. are removed.

Add now the tomatoes and the ketchup.

Stir well again and add the salt.

Let the tomatoes cook well.

Now, add the poppy seeds, blanched almonds, and the saffron strands.

Stir well.

Add the water. Switch off the sauté button. Close the lid of the inner pot and press the chicken button, if there be one. Otherwise, pressure cook for 10 minutes.

Let the Instant Pot cool down on its own.

Open the Instant Pot, add the yogurt and the fried onions.

Press the sauté button and simmer the mixture for about two minutes, uncovered.

That's all. Your exotic *Murg Badami* (Chicken Almond) Curry is now ready.

Prep time: 10 minutes

Cooking time: 20 minutes

Total time: 30 minutes

Note: Different Instant Pot models may have different designs or control options, so please feel free to adapt as you deem fit.

Goan Chicken Xacuti

Pronounced *Shaqooti*, this dish from Goa, Western India bristles with Portuguese influence. The exotic flavors are guaranteed to take your breath away. Try only when you are in a mood for adventure and are NOT too rushed.

Serves 3-4

Ingredients

Whole chicken -1 approx. 800 grams or 28oz or 4 cups (cut into 8 pieces)

Chopped Onion-1

Chopped Ginger- 1 teaspoon

Chopped Garlic-1 teaspoon

Coriander (*Dhania*) powder-1/2 teaspoon

Green Cardamoms (*Chhoti Elaichi*) - 2

Cloves (*Laung*) - 2

Cinnamon (*Dalchinni*) - ½ inch (1 cm.)

Turmeric (*Haldi*) powder- 1 teaspoon

Whole Red Chillies- 2 (deseeded to add flavor and not to make it too hot; you can add more if you desire a really spicy dish.)

Cumin (*Jeera*) seeds-1/2 teaspoon

Desiccated coconut- ½ cup

Poppy seeds (*Khaskhas*) - 3 teaspoons

Fenugreek (*Methi*) seeds- ½ teaspoon

Water-1/2 cup

Salt- 1 teaspoon or to taste

Black Pepper (*Kali Mirch*)- 1 teaspoon (whole)

Cooking Oil- 2 tablespoon

Ghee (Clarified butter)- 1 tablespoon

Lemon juice- 1 tablespoon

Method

Switch on the Instant Pot and press the sauté button.

Dry roast the coriander and cumin seeds in the inner pot till they start changing color and giving off a pleasant aroma.

Remove to a plate.

In the same pot, add the fenugreek seeds and the black pepper (whole) and roast for 2-3 minutes.

Remove to the same plate.

The same way, now roast the poppy seeds and the desiccated coconut till the latter attain a golden brown color.

Remove to the same plate.

Now dry roast the chopped onions till brown.

Note: All the above have to be roasted separately, in batches, because they all have different roasting points. If you roast them all together, some may get burnt while others may NOT be that well-roasted.

Switch off the sauté button.

Now put all the ingredients, except the chicken, lemon juice, and the cooking oil, in a blender and blend well with a little (2 tablespoon) water.

Press the sauté button, and pour in the cooking oil and the *ghee*.

When the oil heats up, add the blended mixture and fry till the oil separates to the sides.

Now add the chicken pieces and mix well.

Fry till the chicken is almost dry.

Switch off the sauté button. Close the lid of the inner pot and press the chicken button, if there be one. Otherwise, pressure cook for 10 minutes.

Let the Instant Pot cool down on its own.

Open the Instant Pot and add the lemon juice.

That's all. Your exotic Goan Chicken Xacuti is ready.

Prep time: 20 minutes (including the dry roast time)

Cooking time: 15 minutes

Total time: 35 minutes

Note: Different Instant Pot models may have different designs or control options, so please feel free to adapt as you deem fit.

Egg Potato Curry

This is a handy dish for the days when you don't have access to any fresh green vegetables. The protein of the eggs is balanced with the carbs from the potatoes and the curry lets you enjoy this dish with a portion of just plain boiled rice.

Serves 3-4

Ingredients

Egg-6 hardboiled and peeled

Potatoes-2 boiled and cut into pieces

Chopped Onion-1

Chopped Ginger-1-inch

Chopped Garlic-4 cloves

Chopped Tomatoes-3

Garam Masala-1/2 teaspoon

Tip: If you can't get ready-made *garam masala* mixture from a nearby Indian store, you can make yours by using 1 black cardamom, 3 green cardamoms, 4 cloves, and 1-inch cinnamon—all ground together for this dish.

Turmeric powder (*Haldi*)-1/2 teaspoon

Red Chilli powder -1/4 teaspoon (This quantity only adds some flavor but does not make the food hot. You may add more if you so prefer.)

Tomato Ketchup-1 tablespoon

Cooking Oil-2 tablespoon

Water-1 cup

Salt- 1 teaspoon or to taste

Method

In a blender, blend together the chopped onion, ginger, garlic, and tomatoes and make into a fine paste.

Turn on the Instant Pot. Press the sauté button.

In the inner pot, add the cooking oil.

When the oil becomes hot, add the hard-boiled eggs and fry gently.

Remove the eggs from oil and keep them on a plate.

Add the onion+ ginger + garlic + tomato paste to the same oil.

Fry well till you get a pleasant aroma from the paste.

Add the rest of the ingredients and stir well.

Now, add the eggs, boiled potatoes with a cup of water, and salt.

When this mixture comes to a boil, turn off the sauté button.

That's all. Your delicious Egg Potato Curry is ready.

Prep time: 10 minutes

Cooking time: 10 minutes

Total time: 20 minutes

Note: Different Instant Pot models may have different designs or control options, so please feel free to adapt as you deem fit.

Basic Indian Mutton Curry

This is the Basic Indian Mutton Curry that once mastered can be easily adapted into a number of variations simply by adding or deleting some ingredients. It is the East Indian version from the states of Bihar and Bengal that we present here.

Serves 3-4

Ingredients

Mutton pieces-1 kg (2 lbs) (4 cups)

Chopped Onions-3 large

Chopped Ginger-2-inch piece

Chopped Garlic-8 Cloves

Chopped Tomatoes-3

Coriander (*Dhania*) powder-2 teaspoon

Turmeric powder (*Haldi*)-1 teaspoon

Garam Masala-1 teaspoon

Tip: If you can't get ready-made *garam masala* mixture from a nearby Indian store, you can make yours by using 1 black cardamom, 3 green cardamoms, 4 cloves, and 1- inch cinnamon—all ground together for this dish.

Red Chilli powder-1/4 teaspoon (just for flavor and not to make it hot; you can add more if you like it hot)

Cumin seeds (*Jeera*)-1/2 teaspoon

Tomato Ketchup-2 tablespoon

Cooking Oil-3 tablespoon

Ghee (Clarified butter)-1 tablespoon

Water-3 cups

Salt- 1 teaspoon or to taste

Method

Switch on the Instant Pot and press the sauté button.

In the inner pot, add the oil.

As the oil turns hot, add the cumin seeds, and let them splutter.

Immediately add the chopped onion.

Stir well till the onions become translucent.

Now, add the chopped ginger and garlic and stir till it all starts giving off a pleasant aroma.

Add the mutton pieces and the *ghee* (clarified butter).

Stir well.

Add the coriander powder, turmeric, *garam masala*, and red chilli powder.

Stir and cook the mutton till all the water evaporates, and the mutton becomes almost dry. This process ensures that all the raw flavors of mutton, onions, etc. are removed.

Add now the tomatoes and the ketchup.

Stir well again and add the salt.

Let the tomatoes cook well.

Now, add the water, and switch off the sauté button.

Close the lid and press the meat/lamb button, if available. Otherwise, pressure cook for 20 minutes.

Let the Instant Pot cool down on its own.

That's all. Your basic Indian Mutton Curry is now ready.

Prep time: 7 minutes

Cooking time: 30 minutes

Total time: 37 minutes

Note: Different Instant Pot models may have different designs or control options, so please feel free to adapt as you deem fit.

Bihari Mutton Curry

This is a very popular dish from the East Indian state of Bihar.

Serves 3-4

Ingredients

Mutton pieces-1 kg (2 lbs) (4 cups)

Onions-3 large (chopped)

Ginger-2-inch piece

Garlic-8 Cloves

Tomatoes-3 (chopped)

(Onion + Ginger + Garlic + Tomatoes blended and made into a fine paste)

Onions-2 finely sliced (please note this is in addition to the onion used for making the paste)

Coriander powder (*Dhania*)-2 teaspoon

Turmeric (*Haldi*)-1 teaspoon

Garam Masala-1 teaspoon

Tip: If you can't get ready-made *garam masala* mixture from a nearby Indian store, you can make yours by using 1 black cardamom, 3 green cardamoms, 4 cloves, and 1- inch cinnamon—all ground together for this dish.

Red Chilli powder-1/4 teaspoon (just for flavor and not to make it hot; you can add more if you like it hot)

Cumin seeds (*Jeera*)-1/2 teaspoon

Cooking Oil-3 tablespoon

Ghee (Clarified butter)-2 tablespoon

Plain unsweetened Yogurt—1/2 cup

Water-3 cups

Sugar-1/2 teaspoon

Salt- 1 teaspoon or to taste

Fresh Coriander leaves (*Dhania Patta*)—Optional for garnishing

Method

Marinate the mutton pieces with all the ingredients EXCEPT *ghee*, onion slices, cumin seeds, and water for an hour.

Switch on the Instant Pot and press the sauté button.

In the inner pot, add the *ghee,* and let it warm up.

As the *ghee* turns hot, add the cumin seeds, and let them splutter.

Add the sliced onion and fry till translucent.

Immediately add the mutton along with all the mixture it has been marinated in.

Stir well till the paste starts giving off a pleasant aroma, and you can see the oil ooze out from the sides. This takes a while; so please have patience.

Cook the mutton till all the water evaporates, and the mutton becomes somewhat dry.

Now, add the water.

Switch off the sauté button. Close the lid of the inner pot and press the meat/lamb button, if there be one. Otherwise, pressure cook for 25 minutes.

Let the Instant Pot cool down on its own.

Open the lid and garnish with coriander leaves before serving.

That's all. Your Bihari Mutton Curry is ready.

Prep time: 10 minutes

Cooking time: 40 minutes

Total time: 50 minutes

Note: Different Instant Pot models may have different designs or control options, so please feel free to adapt as you deem fit.

Yakhni (Mutton cooked in a Yogurt curry)

This is a timeless dish for all ages from Kashmir, the northern most state of India that you will find served in homes as well as restaurants in Kashmir with equal felicity.

Yakhni is usually made with mutton. But there are vegetarian versions too using "nadru" (lotus stem) or even bottle gourd. Interestingly, this dish uses no tomatoes, turmeric, or chillies. The Kashmiri Hindu version, in fact, doesn't even use onions and garlic!

Kashmiris believe that *Yakhni* originally came from Persia, and probably reached Kashmir through the Moghul emperors, viz. Akbar, Jahangir, and Shahjahan, who were all so very fond of Kashmir. The earliest documented recipe, in fact, is found in *Ain-I-Akbari* (the biography of Akbar).

Yakhni may be a corruption of *Akhni*, which means broth or *shorba*. I have tasted its Turkish version in Istanbul and was surprised to learn that it is the Turks' favorite comfort food. They call it *Yayla Çorbası* or meadow soup. Some also call it the White soup (*aks corbası*), or yogurt soup (*yoğurt corbası*). All three versions are made with rice, chicken stock, egg, flour etc. which the Kashmiris don't use.

The only similarity with the Kashmiri version then is the use of yogurt and mint.

I present here the Kashmiri version which I believe is tastier too.

Serves 3-4

Ingredients

Mutton pieces-1 kg (2 lbs) (4 cups)

Thickly Chopped Onions large-3

Finely Sliced Onions large-2

Chopped Ginger-2 inch

Chopped Garlic-6 cloves

Brown Cardamom (*Badi elaichi*)-4

Cinnamon (*Dalchinni*)-3 one inch sticks

Plain unsweetened Yogurt-1/2 kg (18oz) (2 cups)

Chick pea flour-2 tablespoon

Fennel (*Saunf*) powder-1/2 teaspoon

Dried Ginger powder-1/2 teaspoon

Bay Leaf (*Tej patta*)-4

Mint Leaves (*Pudina*)-15 or 20 leaves

Clarified Butter (*ghee*)-1 tablespoon

Salt to taste

Water-1 + ½ cups

Method

Switch on the Instant Pot.

In the inner pot, put the mutton pieces, salt, thickly chopped onions, garlic, ginger, brown cardamom, cinnamon, and water. Close the lid and press the meat/lamb button, if there be one. Otherwise, pressure cook for 20 minutes.

Meanwhile, in a bowl, beat the yogurt, chickpea flour, fennel powder and dried ginger powder well. Add the bay leaves.

Once the mutton cooks, remove the pieces along with the stock to a separate bowl. Separate the onion, ginger, and garlic pieces and make these into a fine paste in a blender.

Pour the yogurt mixture in the inner pot and press the sauté button. Stir till the mixture becomes almost dry.

Switch off the Instant Pot.

Add the onion+ ginger + garlic paste and the mutton stock to the yogurt mixture.

Add the mutton pieces and the mint leaves. Press the sauté button and let it all cook for about 10 minutes.

Separately in a pan, fry the finely sliced onions in the clarified butter till it takes on a nice brown color. Pour the onions along with the clarified butter on to the mutton dish. In case, you don't want to add onions, you can just add the clarified butter to the dish which will still enhance the flavor even though not fully.

That's all. Your *Yakhni* is ready and tastes excellent with plain rice.

Prep time: 5 minutes

Cooking time: 30 minutes

Total time: 35 minutes

Note: Different Instant Pot models may have different designs or control options, so please feel free to adapt as you deem fit.

Khubani Gosht (Mutton with Apricots)

This is another Kashmiri mutton dish, but one which is rarely served in restaurants.

Serves 3-4

Ingredients

Mutton pieces-1 kg (2 lbs) (4 cups)

Chopped Onions-3 large

Chopped Ginger-2-inch piece

Chopped Garlic-8 Cloves

Chopped Tomatoes-3

Turmeric (*Haldi*) powder-1 teaspoon

Garam Masala-1 teaspoon

Tip: If you can't get ready-made *garam masala* mixture from a nearby Indian store, you can make yours by using 1 black cardamom, 3 green cardamoms, 4 cloves, and 1-inch cinnamon—all ground together for this dish.

Red Chilli powder-1/4 teaspoon (just for flavor and not to make it hot; you can add more if you like it hot)

Cumin (*Jeera*) seeds-1/2 teaspoon

Saffron (*Kesar*) strands- 8 or ½ teaspoon (dissolved in 2 tablespoon hot water)

Dried apricots (*Khubani*) - 1 cup (soaked overnight and deseeded)

Tomato Ketchup-2 tablespoon

Cooking Oil-2 tablespoon

Ghee (Clarified butter)-1 tablespoon

Water-1 cup

Salt- 1 teaspoon or to taste

Method

Switch on the Instant Pot and press the sauté button.

In the inner pot, add the oil.

As the oil heats up, add the cumin seeds, and let them splutter.

Immediately add the chopped onion.

Stir well till the onions become translucent.

Now, add the chopped ginger and garlic, and stir till these start giving off a pleasant aroma.

Add the mutton pieces and the *ghee* (clarified butter).

Stir well.

Add the turmeric powder, garam masala, and the red chilli powder.

Stir and cook the mutton till all the water evaporates, and the mutton becomes almost dry. This process ensures that all the raw flavors of mutton, onions, etc. are removed.

Add now the tomatoes and the ketchup.

Stir well again and add the salt.

Let the tomatoes cook well.

Add the soaked apricots and the saffron strands along with the water the saffron was soaked in.

Switch off the sauté button. Now add water, close the lid and press the meat/lamb button, if there be one. Otherwise, pressure cook for 20 minutes.

Let the Instant Pot cool down on its own.

That's all. Your *Khubani Gosht* or Mutton with Apricots is now ready.

Prep time: 7 minutes

Cooking time: 30 minutes

Total time: 37 minutes

Note: Different Instant Pot models may have different designs or control options, so please feel free to adapt as you deem fit.

Mutton "Ishtew" Mughlai

This is the low-calorie version of the very popular mutton dish that you'd find almost everywhere in the areas around Jama Masjid in old Delhi, or in restaurants like Karim's sprinkled all-over Delhi.

Serves 3-4

Ingredients

Mutton pieces-1 kg (2 lbs) (4 cups)

Onions chopped finely-1 kg (2 lbs) (4 cups)

Tomatoes chopped-1 kg (2 lbs) (4 cups)

Garlic chopped-8 cloves

Ginger chopped-2-inch piece

Green Cardamom (*Chhoti Elaichi*)-4

Brown Cardamom (*Badi Elaichi*)-2

Cinnamon (*Dalchinni*)-1-inch stick

Cloves (*Laung*)-6

Bay Leaves (*Tejpatta*)-2

Almonds (Blanched)—15-20

(To blanch almonds, immerse them in half a cup of hot water for 30 minutes. Remove the skin thereafter.)

Cumin Seeds (*Jeera*)-1 teaspoon

Yogurt unsweetened (Indian set curd is preferred)-200 grams (7oz) (1 cup)

Cooking Oil-4 tablespoon

Salt- 1 teaspoon or to taste

Method

Marinate the mutton pieces with yogurt and salt for half an hour.

Switch on the Instant Pot and press the sauté button.

Add the cooking oil in the inner pot.

As soon as the oil warms up, add the cardamom, bay leaves, cinnamon, cloves, and the cumin seeds. Let them brown for a few seconds.

Add the garlic and ginger and again let the mixture roast for a minute. Also add the blanched almonds.

Add the mutton pieces along with the marinade and stir well.

Cover the mutton first with the onions and then with the tomatoes. DO NOT STIR. This is because the mutton has to cook in the juice of the onions and the tomatoes and if we stir at this moment, then the onions and tomatoes will get fried (a result that we don't want).

Switch off the sauté button.

Close the lid and press the meat/lamb button, if available. Otherwise, pressure cook for 20 minutes.

Let the Instant Pot cool down on its own before you open it.

Now press the sauté button, and dry the mixture till it becomes like a thick curry.

That's all. Your Mutton 'Ishtew' Mughlai is ready.

Prep time: 10 minutes (excluding marination time)

Cooking time: 30 minutes

Total time: 40 minutes

Note: Different Instant Pot models may have different designs or control options, so please feel free to adapt as you deem fit.

Mutton Chettinad (Mutton Cooked in a Rich Coconut Curry)

This is a classic recipe from South India that is served on special occasions in the Chettinad region of Tamil Nadu. Liberal use of *garam masala* imparts a gourmet twist to this venerated dish.

The dish bristles with the goodness of coconut milk and coconut powder, while the typical "South Indian" taste comes from *Rai* (black mustard seeds) and curry leaves.

Serves 3-4

Ingredients

Mutton pieces-1 kg (2 lbs) (4 cups)

Onion-1 large (chopped)

Ginger-1-inch piece

Garlic-6 Cloves

Tomatoes-2 (chopped)

(Onion + Ginger + Garlic + Tomatoes blended and made into a fine paste)

Coriander (*Dhania*) powder-2 teaspoon

Turmeric powder (*Haldi*)-1 teaspoon

Garam Masala-1 teaspoon

Tip: If you can't get ready-made *garam masala* mixture from a nearby Indian store, you can make yours by using 1 black cardamom, 3 green cardamoms, 4 cloves, and 1- inch cinnamon—all ground together for this dish.

Red Chilli powder-1/4 teaspoon (just for flavor and not to make it hot; you can add more if you like it hot)

Coconut Milk-200 ml (1 cup approximately)

Desiccated coconut-3 tablespoon

Tamarind paste- 1 tablespoon

Black Mustard seeds (*Rai*) -1/2 teaspoon

Curry leaves-few (around 20)

Cooking Oil -3 tablespoon (Use a milder flavored oil such as groundnut, sesame, or coconut for the best effect)

Salt- 1 teaspoon or to taste

Sugar- ½ teaspoon

Water-1/2 cup (roughly 150 ml)

Method

Switch on the Instant Pot and press the sauté button.

In the inner pot DRY ROAST the desiccated coconut and the coriander powder till the coconut turns a nice golden color.

Remove the DRY ROASTED ingredients on to a plate.

Now add the oil.

As the oil heats up, add the black mustard seeds, and let them splutter.

Immediately add the Onion + Ginger + Garlic + Tomatoes fine paste.

Add the curry leaves and stir well till the paste starts giving off a pleasant aroma, and you can see the oil ooze out from the sides.

Add the mutton pieces and stir well.

Add the turmeric, garam masala, and the red chilli powder.

Cook the mutton till all the water evaporates, and the mutton is rendered dry. Add the salt, sugar, and DRY ROASTED desiccated coconut and coriander powder.

Stir well.

Add water.

Close the lid and press the meat/lamb button or pressure cook for 20 minutes.

Let the Instant Pot cool down on its own.

Open the Instant Pot.

Press the sauté button, and add the coconut milk and tamarind paste.

Bring the mixture to a boil. Switch off the Instant Pot.

That's all. Your classic Mutton Chettinad is ready.

Prep time: 10 minutes

Cooking time: 30 minutes

Total time: 40 minutes

Note: Different Instant Pot models may have different designs or control options, so please feel free to adapt as you deem fit.

Chapter 9: Dessert Recipes

But I, when I undress me

Each night, upon my knees

Will ask the Lord to bless me

With apple-pie and cheese.

— Eugene Field

Sorry Mr. Field, but if you need to taste Indian desserts, you will have to forget apple and cured cheese to start with.

You can sure have cream, milk, and fresh cottage cheese. You can use exotic spices like saffron and green cardamom. You can also use almost any grain or nuts. But just apple and cheese is not enough to please any Indian sweet tooth, sorry.

Why? Because having discovered sugar (or jaggery) from sugar cane, Indians are a little conservative about their sweetmeats. Their desserts have to be SWEET, in all senses of the term.

Their conceit may be pardoned. Because when the sweetest thing that the world knew was honey or raisins, ancient Greek writers from the days of Herodotus and Alexander were marveling about those magical "reeds" in India that could yield a substance that would be sweeter than honey.

So it is established that sugar from sugarcane was gifted to the world by India. Even the knowhow of sugarcane cultivation and processing was spread (mostly forcibly!) to all parts of the world, from Mauritius to the Caribbean, by the British through Indian workers.

It is natural, therefore, to expect that all regions of India would have a very strong dessert making tradition. Sweets have to be offered to gods and exchanged among friends on all auspicious occasions. Any good news, even in corporate offices, would result in a clamor for some exchange of sweets, much to the bewilderment and bemusement of the non-Indians around that place. Celebrating with sweets is something that comes naturally to all Indians.

India is a sub-continent of languages, cultures, and traditions that are intertwined yet independent. Each state or region has something entirely different and wonderful to offer. And there is no better way of learning about their specialties and idiosyncrasies than by savoring their delicacies.

Indian sweets, especially in Northern India, are often called *Mithai.* This is derived from the word *mitha* meaning sweet. It is interesting that some popular Indian street food desserts like *Gulab Jamuns* or *Jalebis* are deep fried (like doughnuts)! The reason could be because oil acts as some kind of preservative for such street food which, unlike home-cooked meals, doesn't normally go into a fridge.

Most of such sweetmeats, as anywhere else in the world, would be prepared by *Halwais* (professional sweet makers) in commercial outlets. So a "Home Style" tradition of making desserts should legitimately raise some eyebrows.

Why, as elsewhere, this craft of making desserts at home has still not died out in India? We asked around and learnt that the first reason is the older generation's mistrust of anything commercial. So, if you want to ensure that whatever ingredients you are using are unadulterated, especially when you are making sweets for an auspicious occasion, you will make these with your very own hands.

The second, more practical reason is that this is the only way to regulate the sugar content or to enable the use of sugar substitutes in your desserts. Yes, you can use your favorite sugar-substitute, like Aspartame (Equal) or Sucralose (Splenda) or Stevia in most Indian desserts except those that require the use of a sugar syrup (like *Jalebi* or *Gulab Jamun*).

The third reason is that Indian sweets are healthier. They generally don't contain eggs; so no bad cholesterol for you. They NEVER use butter or cream or white flour in such big proportions as western cakes or pastries do. They can use veggies like cauliflower or bottle gourd or even lentils and legumes. Consequently, they have better protein and vitamin content than most western style desserts.

In this backdrop, I present a sample of four desserts made from legumes, semolina, coconut, and cottage cheese (paneer).

For more dessert recipes, please feel free to refer to my book "The Ultimate Guide to Cooking Desserts the Indian Way" that has 70 such recipes.

Besan Halva (Chickpea Flour Dessert)

This dessert is fit for the gods, literally, and so is offered quite frequently in temples.

Serves 3-4

Ingredients

Chickpea flour (*Besan*)-1 cup

Sugar-1/2 cup

Clarified butter (*Ghee*)-1/4 cup

Milk-1 cup

Saffron-few strands dissolved in milk

Green Cardamom-2 crushed

Cashew nuts-25 grams (1oz) (1 + 1/2 tablespoon)

Raisins-25 grams (1oz) (1 + 1/2 tablespoon)

Method

Turn on the Instant Pot.

Press the sauté button.

In the inner pot, add the clarified butter.

As soon as the clarified butter warms up, add the *besan* (Chickpea flour) and cashew nuts and stir till these become light brown and give off a lovely aroma.

Do please ensure that you don't burn the flour!

Add the sugar, milk along with the saffron, the cardamom, and raisins to the flour.

Stir well till the dessert (*halva*) dries up.

That's all. Your *Besan Halva* is ready.

Prep time: 5 minutes

Cooking time: 7 minutes

Total time: 12 minutes

Note: Different Instant Pot models may have different designs or control options, so please feel free to adapt as you deem fit.

Suji Halva (Semolina Dessert)

This one is offered as *prasadam* outside Hindu temples or Sikh Gurudwaras throughout the world free-of-charge and certainly tastes divine.

Serves 3-4

Ingredients

Semolina (*Suji*)-1 cup

Sugar-1/2 cup

Clarified butter (*Ghee*)-1/4 cup

Milk-1 cup

Saffron-few strands dissolved in milk

Green cardamom-2 crushed

Method

Turn on the Instant Pot.

Press the sauté button.

In the inner pot, add the clarified butter.

As soon as the clarified butter warms up, add the semolina (*Suji*) and stir till it becomes light brown and gives off a lovely aroma.

Do please ensure that you don't burn the semolina!

Add the sugar and the milk along with the saffron and the cardamom to the semolina.

Stir well till the dessert (*halva*) dries up.

That's all. Your *Suji ka Halva* is ready.

Prep time: 5 minutes

Cooking time: 7 minutes

Total time: 12 minutes

Note: Different Instant Pot models may have different designs or control options, so please feel free to adapt as you deem fit.

Narial Barfi in a JIFFY (Short-cut Coconut Barfi)

When you want to have home-made coconut *barfi* but don't have the time to make the classic version ...

Serves 3-4

Ingredients

Sweetened condensed milk: 1 cup (250 grams)

Desiccated coconut- 2 cups (500 grams)

Green cardamom- 2 crushed

Method

Turn on the Instant Pot.

Press the sauté button.

In the inner pot, mix together all the ingredients mentioned above.

Keep on stirring till the mixture is dry.

Switch off the Instant Pot.

Pour this mixture on to a flat plate.

Let the mixture cool. You can now cut small pieces (in whatever shape you desire) and enjoy.

That's all. Your *Narial Barfi in a JIFFY* is ready.

Prep time: 5 minutes

Cooking time: 10 minutes

Total time: 15 minutes

Note: Different Instant Pot models may have different designs or control options, so please feel free to adapt as you deem fit.

Sandesh (Cottage Cheese Sweet)

This is the classic Eastern Indian sweetmeat that Bengalis are so fond of. Western palates too may enjoy its moderate sweet taste more.

Serves 3-4

Ingredients

Fresh *Paneer* (cottage cheese)-1/2 kg (18oz) (2 cups)

Sugar-250 grams (9oz) (1 cup)

Milk Powder–3 tablespoons

Rose water-2 tablespoons

Rose essence- 2 drops

Red food color- 2 drops (optional)

Method

In the inner pot, mix together all the ingredients, EXCEPT rose water, rose essence, and food color.

Turn on the Instant Pot.

Press the sauté button.

Keep stirring till all the water dries up and the consistency becomes thick.

Switch off the Instant Pot.

Add the rose water, rose essence, and food color.

Pour the content into a food processor and blend well.

Pour the mixture into a big plate or serving dish and let it cool down.

Now pick up small portions and make it into any shape with your hands or by using any mold.

That's all. Your basic *Sandesh* is ready.

Note: Feel free to substitute rose water/essence/color with any other flavor (like saffron, cardamom, vanilla, orange...) and color of your choice.

Prep time: 5 minutes

Cooking time: 10 minutes

Total time: 15 minutes

Note: Different Instant Pot models may have different designs or control options, so please feel free to adapt as you deem fit.

Chapter 10: An Introduction to Some Basic Indian Spices

It is easy to be overwhelmed with the sheer number and variety of fresh herbs and spices that are commonly used in Indian cuisine. I shouldn't, therefore, make this topic even more complicated by giving the scientific or botanical names of such spices, or where they grow, or how these are harvested and processed. There are many excellent books who have done better justice to this topic.

What I shall attempt here is to just list out some twenty of these spices that you should experiment with when you are just starting out with "Home Style" Indian cooking. The ones in **bold** are essential for any authentic Indian kitchen. The rest are optional.

The discerning reader may notice the omission of *Kastoori Methi* (a very fragrant variety of Fenugreek) which is very popular for making curries in Indian restaurants. That's precisely the reason why I am leaving this out from my list. But if you prefer your food to taste like *dhaba* food, do stock on *Kastoori Methi* too. Just remember that this is such a strong herb that it will drown the fragrance of all other spices, howsoever expensive they may be. So for heavens, don't use your saffron with *Kastoori Methi* ever!

I am also leaving out some expensive spices like nutmeg or star aniseed as they are hardly ever used in your day-to-day cooking.

Here is then my list, in alphabetical order.

Amchur (Dried green mango powder): This is used for imparting a strong sour taste.

Asafoetida (Hing): This is used in small quantities for imparting a strong smell. It is considered very healthy for digestive purposes though some people may find the smell unpleasant and strong. Don't use your saffron with *Hing*, therefore, ever!

Bay Leaves (Tej Patta): Used as a flavoring agent.

Cardamom (Elaichi): These come in two varieties: one is small, pale-green and the other is large and brown/black. The pale green variety is used in many Indian dishes including desserts. The brown variety is used for making curries or *pulaos*, but not in sweetmeats.

Chilli (Kashmiri Red variety): In our recipes, we have suggested the use of Kashmiri Red Chillies as these impart a nice red color and are not as hot as are the other red chillies. In case, you like your food to be really hot, then you can use the other red chillies available in the market which are much hotter.

Cinnamon (Dalchini): This looks like the thin bark of a tree and imparts a lovely flavor both to the sweet and curried dishes. In India, however, it is more used for curries as Indians like Cardamom in their desserts much more than Cinnamon.

Cloves (Laung): These look like dried flower buds and add a lovely flavor to the food. Cloves are supposed to have antiseptic qualities which helps preserve food.

Coconut (Narial) powder or milk: This is used commonly in many South Indian and coastal Indian preparations.

Coriander seeds and fresh green leaves (Dhania and Dhania patta): The dried seeds of Coriander form an essential part of Indian curries and are used quite extensively. The fresh green leaves are used for making *Chutneys* (Indian sauce) as well as for sprinkling on curries. Since the fresh leaves have a strong flavor, they should only be used by those who really like them.

Cumin seeds (Jeera): Cumin is another essential ingredient of Indian cuisine and is generally the first spice to go into the heated cooking oil before other items are added.

Curry leaves (Kare-patta): These leaves have a lovely flavor and are absolutely essential if you like South Indian cuisine. In India, it grows in abundance and so is easily the cheapest herb to use. Generally used fresh, these can also be dried and used as they retain much of their fragrance even in the dried form.

Fennel (Saunf): This is used for making some dishes and forms a part of the *Pachphoran* (which shall be discussed later).

Fenugreek (Methi): These are small flat seeds which have a slightly bitter flavor and must be used only in the quantities prescribed. They add quite a piquant flavor to the curries or dry dishes they are added to which is liked by many Indians. Lately, Fenugreek has acquired quite a cult status because of its almost magical effect in reducing the severity of Diabetes.

Garam Masala: This is a mixture in equal quantities of cinnamon, cloves, cardamom (both pale-green and brown variety) and whole black pepper corns. These can be ground together and kept in air-tight containers for future use for up to a week. Some dishes can also be made by putting the whole spices in oil/ clarified butter (*Ghee*).

All lovers of Indian cooking must learn to use this mixture properly. If you cook Indian dishes only occasionally, you may be tempted to use the commercially available *Garam Masala* powders. Please remember, however, that to economize on costs, some manufacturers skimp on the more expensive ingredients mentioned above and instead add lots of coriander powder, cumin powder, turmeric powder, red chilli powder etc. to add volume. They even add *Kastoori Methi* which just drowns the subtle flavors of other *Garam Masalas*. So, do check before you buy such a ready mix of spices.

Mustard seeds black (Rai): These are black mustard seeds which look the same as the yellow variety but are supposed to be more pungent than their yellow cousins. This mustard seed is used a lot in South Indian and Western Indian cooking.

Onion seeds dried (Mangrela or Kalonji): This spice is generally used as a part of the *Pachphoran* (which is discussed on the next page).

Pachphoran: Literally, a mixture of five spices namely black mustard seeds, cumin seeds, fenugreek seeds, fennel seeds, and dried onion seeds, mixed in equal proportion, this category is regularly used in quite a few Eastern Indian dishes.

Saffron (Kesar): Easily the most expensive spice in the world, this comes from the stamen of the saffron flower. It has thread like strands in a dark orange color which when dissolved in milk or water gives out its color along with its mild, earthy flavor. Not a spice to be used casually, saffron is used mostly in making desserts and some exotic dishes.

Turmeric (Haldi): This is easily the commonest and the most important ingredient in any Indian curry dish. Though it does not have much of a flavor, it has a dark yellow color and a lot of therapeutic value.

Yogurt (Dahi): Not really a spice or herb, yogurt is frequently used in many Indian dishes. The variety used in cooking is cultured yogurt and is always unflavored. That way it comes closest to the Greek variety of yogurt.

Other books by Prasenjeet Kumar

Cookbooks

HOME STYLE INDIAN COOKING IN A JIFFY

HOW TO COOK IN A JIFFY EVEN IF YOU HAVE NEVER BOILED AN EGG BEFORE

HEALTHY COOKING IN A JIFFY: THE COMPLETE NO FAD NO DIET HANDBOOK

HOW TO CREATE A COMPLETE MEAL IN A JIFFY

THE ULTIMATE GUIDE TO COOKING LENTILS THE INDIAN WAY

THE ULTIMATE GUIDE TO COOKING RICE THE INDIAN WAY

THE ULTIMATE GUIDE TO COOKING FISH THE INDIAN WAY

THE ULTIMATE GUIDE TO COOKING CHICKEN THE INDIAN WAY

THE ULTIMATE GUIDE TO COOKING VEGETABLES THE INDIAN WAY

THE ULTIMATE GUIDE TO COOKING DESSERTS THE INDIAN WAY

FICTION by Prasenjeet Kumar

LEGALLY IN LOVE

LOVE KARMA CROSSED

WHEN GANGES MET THE NORTH SEA

YOU CAN'T KILL MY LOVE: A KASHMIR HOLOCAUST LOVE STORY

AUTISTICALLY YOURS

STILL MISSING...

WHEN YOU CAN'T TRUST LOVE

THE ENEMY WITHIN

THE SCEPTIC

FICTION by Arun Kumar and Prasenjeet Kumar

KASHMIR IS FREE

KASHMIR THINKS ITS FREE

Books by Sonali Kumar and Prasenjeet Kumar

THE OUTSIDER'S CURSE

THE OUTSIDER'S TALES

Books by Prasenjeet Kumar for Introverts in the "Quiet Phoenix" Series

CELEBRATING QUIET PEOPLE: UPLIFTING STORIES FOR INTROVERTS AND HIGHLY SENSITIVE PERSONS

QUIET PHOENIX: AN INTROVERT'S GUIDE TO RISING IN CAREER & LIFE

QUIET PHOENIX 2: FROM FAILURE TO FULFILMENT: A MEMOIR OF AN INTROVERTED CHILD

CELEBRATING QUIET LEADERS: UPLIFTING STORIES OF INTROVERTED LEADERS WHO CHANGED HISTORY

CELEBRATING QUIET ARTISTS: STIRRING STORIES OF INTROVERTED ARTISTS THE WORLD CAN'T FORGET

Books by Prasenjeet Kumar in the "Self-Publishing WITHOUT SPENDING A DIME" Series

HOW TO BE AN AUTHOR ENTREPRENEUR WITHOUT SPENDING A DIME

HOW TO TRANSLATE YOUR BOOKS WITHOUT SPENDING A DIME

HOW TO MARKET YOUR BOOKS WITHOUT SPENDING A DIME

HOW TO HAVE A HAPPIER WRITER MINDSET WITHOUT SPENDING A DIME

Connect with the Authors

Feel free to visit us at: http://www.cookinginajiffy.com

Should you have any questions or comments, please do not hesitate to write to us anytime at ciaj@cookinginajiffy.com.

We would also love to connect with you on Social Media. Join us on:

Twitter

https://twitter.com/CookinginaJiffy

Goodreads

https://www.goodreads.com/prasenjeet

Google Plus

https://www.google.com/+PrasenjeetKumarAuthor

About the Authors

Prasenjeet Kumar

Prasenjeet Kumar is the author/co-author of over 33 books in four genres: Fiction, motivational books for introverts (the Quiet Phoenix series), books on Self-Publishing (Self-Publishing WITHOUT SPENDING A DIME series) and cookbooks (Cooking In A Jiffy series). His books (over 60 titles and counting) have been translated into French, German, Italian, Japanese, Spanish, and Portuguese, and sell in over 50 countries.

Prasenjeet is a Law graduate from the University College London (2005-2008), London University and a Philosophy Honours graduate from St. Stephen's College (2002-2005), Delhi University. In addition, he holds a Legal Practice Course (LPC) Diploma from College of Law, Bloomsbury, London, and was for a brief while, a solicitor of England and Wales.

Prasenjeet loves gourmet food, music, films, and travelling. He has already covered twenty-five countries including Canada, China, Denmark, Dubai, Germany, Greece, Hong Kong, Indonesia, Israel, Italy, Jordan, Macau, Malaysia, Mauritius, Montenegro, Nepal, Sharjah, Spain, Sweden, Switzerland, Thailand, Turkey, UK, Uzbekistan, and the USA.

Prasenjeet is the self-taught designer, writer, editor, and proud owner of the website cookinginajiffy.com which he has dedicated to his mother. He also runs another website publishwithprasen.com where he shares tips about writing and self-publishing.

Sonali Kumar

Sonali Kumar retired from the Indian Administrative Service (IAS) after a distinguished service of over 36 years with the Government of India as well as the Government of Jammu and Kashmir.

During this period, she held a number of assignments related to industry and commerce (including Public Sector Undertakings), textiles (handlooms & handicrafts), education, welfare, forests & environment, agriculture, horticulture, co-operatives, rural and urban development, health & medical education, anti-drought prone and anti-desert area development programs, revenue, judicial, and even disaster relief operations.

Sonali believes that her myriad experiences spanning all kinds of sectors have equipped her with the powers of ideation, problem-solving, out-of-box thinking, and strategic policy insights that only a long stint in IAS probably can endow one with.

Post-retirement, Sonali is working with her son Prasenjeet putting out books in the "Cooking In A Jiffy" series. In her spare time, she doesn't mind mentoring or advising people who wish to benefit from her otherwise vast experience in public service.